BLACK BAR

Black Barnsley

A record of grisley deeds done in Barnsley & District from 1664 to 1913

Revised Edition

Ian Harley

Wharncliffe Publishing Limited

First published in 1985
Reprinted in this revised and
updated edition in 1999
by Wharncliffe Publishing Limited
an imprint of
Pen and Sword Books Limited,
47 Church Street, Barnsley,
South Yorkshire. S70 2AS

For up-to-date information on other titles produced under the Wharncliffe imprint, please telephone or write to:

Wharncliffe Publishing Limited
FREEPOST
47 Church Street
Barnsley
South Yorkshire S70 2BR
Telephone (24 hours): 01226 - 734555

ISBN: 1-871647-60-6

A CIP catalogue record of this book is available from the British Library

Printed in Great Britain by
Redwood Books, Trowbridge, Wiltshire

Contents

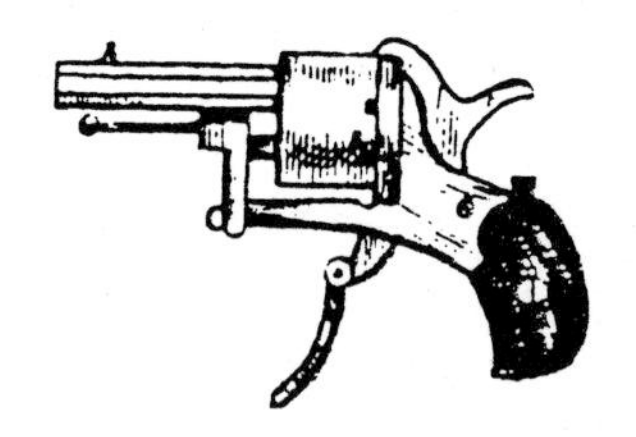

Introduction

BLACK BARNSLEY is not intended as a comprehensive catalogue of violent crimes in the Barnsley area. Indeed such a catalogue would be impossible to produce as many of the area's darkest deeds are shrouded in the mists of time and folklore. It is, however, a record of selected events usually ending in death, which captured the attention and imagination of our forefathers.

To some, this book, prepared from a series written by Ian Harley for the Barnsley Chronicle, borders on the macabre. They would argue that many of the incidents selected for inclusion would have been better left forgotten. But closer examination of the predatory occurrences reveals a great deal about the area and its inhabitants. It tells us how they lived, worked and played in far greater detail than can ever be discovered from meeting reports of the Barnsley Board of Guardians and other erstwhile bodies.

Similarly it gives us information about the respective satellite townships that now combine together under the umbrella of the Barnsley Metropolitan District and to some extent, it tells us how our forefathers made their living, what they wore, what they drank, the buildings they visited at that time and the roads on which they passed.

Even a cursory examination of the profiles can reveal the major part that alcohol played in many of the events, yet readers will also note that many of the inquest hearings were also held in licensed establishments. Public houses, it seems, along with churches, provide the link-lines into the past. They were the public meeting places of the day.

The fact that this book is titled 'black' Barnsley does not mean that Barnsley headed the league tables in violent crime, far from it. For decades prior to 1840 it was a proud boast of

In the 14th century it is known that the family in residence at Cannon Hall were involved in a long-running family feud which involved kidnap and death.

the town that few 'true' Barnsley necks had been offered to the hangman's noose. That however, appears to have been as much through luck as anything else.

Using local place names to delve further back in time, we find evidence to indicate that severe punishment was meted out locally, before York became the execution centre of the North.

One example of this is around the site of the former police station at the Hoyland Common end of Birdwell. The telephone kiosk there and the name of a commercial vehicle export firm's premises, denote that the area was once known as 'Hangmanstone'. It is well known that perpetrators of vile deeds in the days prior to official judicial hearings, often suffered execution in public places and the Hangmanstone area then occupied a prominent road junction.

Rumour has it that William Elmhirst, the surgeon-apothecary and vet who pioneered innoculation against smallpox lived locally at Genn House, Worsbrough and died when his horse shied at a corpse lying in the road at Hangmanstone Bar in 1773. Unfortunately the rumour cannot be substantiated.

Likewise it is known that an area of Barnsley around New Street and Wood Street was for many years, known simply as the 'Barebones'. Most local historians believe that the area gained its nickname from the fact that a gibbet was once sited there.

It is also well known that Barnsley Common, now forming Locke Park and part of Kingstone, contained a piece of land known as 'Gallows Hill'. The 19th century Dodworth Green writer, John Hobson, wrote in his journal that rumour had it that a woman by the name of Frudd was executed there in the early 1700s, for the theft of a silver spoon, a crime of which she was later proved innocent.

Whether any of those localities really saw executions cannot be confirmed but it is certain that Barnsley had its share of wrongdoers from early times.

In 1362 a prominent member of the Rockley family of Worsbrough, Sir Adam de Everingham was ex-communicated for 'laying violent hands' on Richard de Halghton at Darfield Church. And just three years later a Waine de Nordel is reputed to have killed John de Staynton in self defence. Also in the 14th century, it is known that the family then in residence at Cannon Hall were involved in a long-running family feud which involved kidnap and death.

1641 appears to have been the year of Barnsley's first recorded violent death. The victim was a cavalry officer by the name of Gervase White who was stationed in Barnsley as part of a Duke of Newcastle garrison, established during the civil war. Unfortunately it seems the soldiers and the locals did not get on well and White met his death during an affray. The leader of the local faction was a man named Benton, who was duly arrested and committed to York for sentence. There is no record as to his ultimate fate.

Even if Benton did suffer capital punishment, he was not

the first inhabitant of the area to do so. That dubious honour appears to be claimed in 1585 by a native of Penistone, Thomas de Alsco. He was 39 years of age when executed at Tyburn for coining guineas at the premises of Simon Portius, a silversmith of Jubbergate, York.

The year 1680 saw the arrest of a highwayman at Barnsley's Bull Inn, then run by Simon Knowles. Andrew Tucker (29) was later hanged for robbing the mail post at Knaresborough.

Four years later saw the hanging of 43 year-old William Nevison of Wortley for highway robbery and, in August 1753, 22-year-old Thomas Downing of Howbrook, Tankersley, was hanged 'on suspicion of sheep stealing', from one James Bincliff.

Robert Watson (22), believed to have lived in Hoyland, was executed on April 8, 1786, for robbing a yeoman by the name of William Bailes of seven guineas, while he was en route from Rotherham to Barnsley.

By 1795, however, three Barnsley men were in York prison awaiting execution for 'feloniously entering, by means of a false key', the Barnsley premises of Joseph Walker and stealing a quantity of rum. William Hobson, known as the 'gaffer', a canal excavator called James Ward and a winemaker, also by the name of Hobson, managed to reprieve their own lives when they intervened in a 'murderous' attack on a gaoler. Their timely intervention and 'respect for lawful authority', received honourable mention at the Home Office with the result that the winemaker and canal excavator had their sentences commuted to one of deportation. 'Artful Olf Gaffer' Hobson, had his sentence commuted to two years imprisonment and returned to Barnsley, but a further burglary resulted in him also being transported to Australia.

Samuel Booth, the subject of our sixth profile, was executed in 1820 and 'Slenderman', our ninth profile, a few years late. Our forefathers, however, did not consider either of them to be true Barnsleyites and still claimed the town had cheated the gallows of a victim.

That, however, changed in July 1840 when a 67-year-old bleacher, Joseph Marshall, appeared in the dock of York

Assizes. Marshall's crime was not one of murder but rape, committed against a 12-year-old orphan girl by the name of Eliza Middleton, when she was in the house of her stonemason uncle.

Marshall heard the judge tell him: 'You have arrived at the time of life, when ungovernable passions cannot be pleaded as an excuse for your crime.' Crying: 'God have mercy upon me' as he was led away, Marshall was subsequently hanged and Barnsley had lost its proud boast.

Returning to the profiles that follow, they include violent acts from poaches to Earls and from mothers to muggers. Some were mysteries at the time and some remain so today. Some were brutal, others border on accidental . . . All are sad.

The series, researched from library reference books, newspaper files, local historians and museums, ends shortly before the First World War. Continuing the profiles after then could cause embarrassment to surviving relatives, while the loss of human life became all too commonplace an event on the battlefields of the Western Front during World War One.

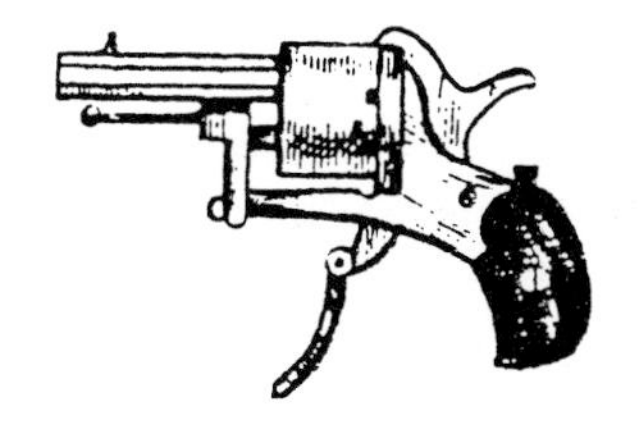

Victim: ***Thomas Wildsmith, run through with sword,*** **1664**

The perpetrator of Barnsley's first recorded murder was a gentleman and attorney, the victim a bailiff and surprisingly, it was probably a murder which gladdened the hearts of some religious members of Barnsley society.

According to a coroner's inquest, the deed took place on May 3 when Cawthorne bailiff Thomas Wildsmith, along with colleagues Richard Wainwright and William Skelton and another unnamed man, were sent to arrest Samuel Wortley and William Hinchliffe for a debt of £300.

The quartet arrived at a public house, believed to have been kept by Hinchliffe, called for a quart of ale and asked to speak to Hinchliffe. When Hinchliffe arrived he was duly arrested. But he and his brother then prevailed on Wildsmith to retire to the parlour where Hinchliffe proposed to give him a bond for £500.

Meanwhile Mrs Hinchliffe had gone to a chamber occupied by a Mr Wortley. Informed about the bailiffs' arrival, Wortley went down to the parlour with a drawn sword or rapier concealed beneath his coat. When the luckless Wildsmith attempted to arrest him also, Wortley turned on him and said: "I will run thee through, thou shalt arrest none of me".

He then made two passes at Wildsmith with his sword, the second of which passed through his body. Opening the parlour door, he pushed Wildsmith through to his colleagues, then slamming and fastening the door he made good his escape.

Despite his wound, Wildsmith remained conscious and told Wainwright: "Ah, Dickie, I am slain".

He was still conscious when Richard Smith, the minister or rather 'perpetual curate', at St Mary's Church, arrived after being summoned to pray with him and for him.

Naming Wortley as his assailant, Wildsmith gasped out: "Ah fye on him. If I had a thousand lives they have all gone."

Wortley's freedom was shortlived after the death of Wildsmith. He was captured, tried at York Assizes but, strange to say, was acquitted despite the fact that Wildsmith's widow begged that he be punished, saying that she had been left with a large family and her husband's debts to pay.

The reason for Wortley's acquittal remains a mystery as indeed does the fact that he owed a substantial sum of money — and to whom? Indeed the fact that his name appears on a subsidy roll for Barnsley in 1663 shows him to be a man of substance in what was then a small and unimportant town. One possible explanation for the bailiffs being sent against him results from the death of the last Sir Francis Wortley of Wortley, without an heir a few months previously.

Sir Francis left his estate to an illegitimate daughter, ignoring the Barnsley branch of his family. They contested the accession and may have won their case, had the illegitimate daughter not married the Honourable Sidney Montagu. Faced with the power and wealth of the Montagu family, the Wortleys of Barnsley made little headway in their claim but faced hefty bills for litigation.

Perhaps even more intriguing is the fact that Wildsmith, the victim, must have been hated by many members of the Quaker faith, a small but important part of Barnsley society.

In 1664 Wildsmith had been responsible for several Quakers being committed to a House of Correction at Wakefield. Others were fined and had their goods seized.

At that time persecution of the Quakers seems to have been quite a popular pastime and Wildsmith was at the forefront of their imprisonment, the spoiling of their goods and the driving off of their cattle. Apparently he had made the boast that he would "live on the Quakers three years and raise his fortune by them".

So when he fell at the end of Wortley's sword so fell the Quakers' biggest local persecutor. Rumour has it that his colleagues took his death as a warning and in future left the Quakers to go about their business virtually unharrassed.

Victim: ***Nicholas Cudworth, axed to death,*** **1672**

Only one account exists concerning the murder of Mr Cudworth and that was only committed to paper many years after the alleged offence took place. It was recorded by Dodworth Green historian, John Hobson in the journal which bears his name. The accuracy of its information relies on the memory of a character by the name of Toby Holland, who wrote to Mr Hobson when he was was 76 years of age in 1729, but he had only been twelve years of age when the alleged foul deed took place.

The victim was a gentleman and the last member of a family named Cudworth, who lived at Worsbrough. The assassin was his son-in-law, a man by the name of Geoffrey Materson. According to the account, Mr Cudworth was walking in the area known as The Closes at Worsbrough, when he met an untimely and bloody end resulting from the blows with an axe, allegedly wielded by Materson. His body was then carried to a quarry and covered with stones.

Unfortunately for Materson, his concealment of the crime was not of the highest standard and part of a garment was later spotted by a woman, who had gone to the quarry to wash clothes in the large pond of water that had gathered there.

With the body uncovered, Materson was apprehended, sent to York, and condemned. But somehow he escaped from custody before execution and fled to Ireland.

The account adds that the Cudworth lands were bought by Justice Edmunds, despite the fact that Mr Cudworth left a widow and at least one son was being brought up with the name of Cudworth.

If you are intrigued by that short account, you're in good company, as several historians over the years have found this crime fascinating. These have included Wilkinson, who hypothesized on the matter after conducting some research of his own; he determined that the Cudworth family did live in Worsbrough for many generations and also owned property at Eastfield, Thurgoland. He found a brass plate in the memory of Nicholas Cudworth on the pulpit of St Mary's Church, Worsbrough Village.

That gentleman died in 1627 after having six sons and four daughters to his first wife, Frances. His second wife, Sarah, was responsible for the remembrance being placed on the pulpit. She did not have any children to him.

With six sons to his credit, not to mention the possibility of nephews and the like, it is logical that there were several Cudworths about when Toby Holland was a boy. And records reveal that a Robert Cudworth was interred in April 1637 and another Nicholas Cudworth in October 1672.

The latter could have been the murder victim although that would have made Toby 18 or 19 at the time of the murder and not twelve as he believed. Neither did the latter death mark the end of the Cudworth family although it could have marked the end of members of the Worsbrough Branch.

It is known that in 1688 one Jonathan Cudworth assigned a house and land for the use of a curate and lecturer in Worsbrough. And he didn't die until 1730.

There you have it then. Was there a murder or wasn't there? It makes a change from asking who the culprit was. The absence of records concerning the alleged murder and subsequent fate of Geoffrey Materson is not unusual in itself although the fact that Materson is supposed to have escaped to the sanctuary of Ireland does make one suspect that he would have been remembered, if only in folklore. What is more suspicious is the fact that only account of these events were written some 60 odd years after the event. One would have thought that there were others, equally as old as Toby Holland, who could have supplied some corroborative information. Allowing for the much smaller population in those days, it could be that others were difficult to find. But information on the incident would only have had to be passed down one generation, from father to son or mother to daughter.

Perhaps the oddest thing about the affair is that if Toby was correct in his dates – why is there no record of a Cudworth family burial around 1765? Conversely, if the second Nicholas Cudworth was the victim – can we rely on the information of an old man whose memory was so bad that he believed that the event took place in his boyhood, when it was actually in the early years of his manhood?

Victim: ***Thomas Maddox, stabbed and bludgeoned,*** **1681**

Although this crime did not occur in Barnsley, the case is an interesting one and was greatly talked about in the town at the time because the offender lived locally and the victim was his boon companion.

Alexander, Earl of Eglinton was a Scottish earl of great influence who, appears to have, first moved to the Barnsley area, on his marriage to the widow, Lady Grace Wentworth, in 1678. The daughter and heiress to Francis Popley Esquire of Woolley Moorhouse, Lady Grace had been married to Sir Thomas Wentworth, who played such an active part in the Civil Wars, until his death in December 1675. An indication of the wealth she inherited from him may be best indicated by the fact that his funeral, which preceded burial at Silkstone Church, cost £1,200 and attracted 4,000 mourners.

After her re-marriage, Lady Grace and Earl Eglinton, were described as living in 'great style and consequence' at Bretton Hall. That was, of course, until the night of January 21st, 1681, when the Earl arrived at Doncaster's Angel Inn with his boon companion, Thomas Maddox, a Barnsley magistrate Jasper Blythman and gentleman Thomas Derby.

Soon the quartet were satisfying their thirst and then called for dice in a box so they could enjoy a game of 'Hazard', a game which was certainly to prove hazardous to Thomas Maddox.

Three times the parties played and three times the noble Earl had to resort to playing 'on tick' before getting back into the black and immediately demanding payment. And each time an argument ensued with Maddox refusing to pay and saying that 'his lord' owed him £3 which he had won in 'the cockpitt'. On the first occasion, the Earl called him a 'dog' and threatened to 'phillipper' him on the nose. But what occurred on the third occasion was far worse than that. The Earl unsheathed his sword and made repeated passes at Maddox despite his plea: 'For Christ's sake, my Lord, bee quiett, here is too much harme done allready'.

Maddox had already suffered at least one serious wound to the thigh by the time the Earl yielded to the intervention of Blythman and Derby, asking them to bear witness that Maddox had run on to the bloodied point. Unfortunately Maddox continued to be threatening and abusive, saying such things as: 'The Scotch dog has wounded me and none but a pittiful Scotch Lord would have done it'.

While one of the peacemakers was engaged in bending to the floor to retrieve the Earl's hat and perriwig, the Earl continued his attack on Maddox – finishing off with a violent blow to the head with his cane. Suffering a serious wound to his left side as well as the injuries to his thigh and head, Maddox did not live long. But even his death failed to make the Earl repentent.

When William Squire, a Doncaster gentleman, was summoned to the scene and refused the Earl's offer of a glass of wine, the Earl heaved up his cane saying he would 'Maddox' him. Perhaps it was the Earl's fate and the working of judicial proceedings, rather than the offence itself, which made the episode such a popular topic of conversion in Barnsley.

The Earl was tried at York, found guilty and sentenced to death after having paid £100 to avoid the stigma of being chained. He was, however, then reprieved 'till the King's pleasure was known' and eventually pardoned and set free without any lands or entitlements being forfeited. Some may say this case showed British Justice to work in different fashions for the nobility and the populace. Others may say the Earl was just lucky.

Certainly he led a full life, living at Bretton with Lady Grace until her death in March 1698. Then, at the age of 70, he married a 90-year-old widow, Katharine St Quentin whose first of four husbands had been Michael Wentworth, son of Sir George Wentworth, Knight of Woolley.

It appears though that Eglinton's luck did not hold for following generations of his line, as his grandson was later shot and killed in a contest with a poaching exciseman.

Victim: ***Clara Wild, drowned, July,*** **1783**

The strange case of Martha or 'Matty' Wild is an intriguing one. For nowhere are there any records that Martha ever stood trial for the heinous murder of her six-months-old daughter, Clara.

It seems our 18th century forebares did not know how to deal with cases of infanticide. They realised that whoever did such things must almost inevitably be mentally unbalanced, but simply did not have the facilities and knowledge to treat them. The unfortunate Martha Wild, therefore, appears to have spent quite some time chained by the leg to a bed in Barnsley's workhouse. Indeed some reports say she ended her life, there while others claim that she was eventually removed to an asylum. All agree that the murder shook the town and that many believed Martha's ghost lived on after her – inhabiting part of the Dearne Valley somewhere in the region of Old Mill and presumably, searching for the baby whose life she so tragically ended.

With no inquest or court records to rely on, the exact date of the crime can only be estimated. Indeed most reports seem to concentrate on what a lady called Peggie Parrington recalled from her childhood, 69 years after the event took place.

If her account is to be believed, the tragic departure of little Clara took place on a Saturday morning in July 1783.

Her story is that Martha was brought up in a dilapidated cottage opposite St Mary's Church in Church Street, Barnsley – just yards away from the site now occupied by the Chronicle offices.

No mention is made of Martha's father, but her mother was Ann Fletcher and she had two brothers, Matthew and George, who both became plasterers. Martha married John Wild, described as a little, bow-legged tailor who lived in the Red Lion yard, Church Street, and together they had four children: Elizabeth, George, Mary and Clara.

Martha, Peggie Parrington reported, always 'went out of her mind when in the family way and was jealous of Johnny.' At such times, she had to be watched.

So it was that Martha carried her baby Clara across Harborough

Hill, walking in the direction of Eymingwood, sometimes written as 'Eaming Wood'. Martha had chased away her son George who had tried to follow her. Minutes later she had drowned the six month old child in a cattle trough at the side of the lane leading to Eymingwood.

Then a man appeared on the scene, got hold of the infant and said: 'Damn thee, what didst thou do it for?'

Martha replied: 'A black man told me', upon which the man shook her and said he would do the same by her which made her cry out.

It was at this point that Peggie Parrington claimed to have arrived

at the scene. At that time she was known as Margaret Winterbottom, and had been bathing in the Cross Hoyle, which was part of the River Dearne, with Honoria Dawes, Elizabeth Pickering of the Red Lion, and Elizabeth and Hannah Fletcher.

They saw people running down the woodside and concluded that something was amiss. Most ran to the scene carrying their shoes and socks but Honoria Dawes was in such a hurry that she arrived there still in the nude.

Johnny Watt, says the account, lamented the death of Clara very much but an unrepentent Martha threatened to kill her other children. She was delivered into the custody of one Richard Woodcock and remained at his house until the Monday, when she was removed to the workhouse. There she was kept in one of four almshouses, chained by her leg to a bed, until 'at length', she was removed to the asylum.

Mr John Widdop, in his *Barnsley and its Superstitions* has the following notice of Martha Wild, 'Anyone crossing from Harborough Hill over the field to Eymingwood corner, and going down the woodside, will find almost buried in the ground a stone trough which nearly overflows in the rainy season.

'In this trough a demented woman named Martha Wild drowned her infant child. The poor woman was confined during the remainder of her life in the old workhouse near St Mary's Church where she was fastened to the bedstead on which she lay.'

'After her death it was averred by many that her spirit could not rest and that it was frequently seen near the trough, as if searching for the drowned child; and this story has obtained credence even amongst grown men.

'Just as the wood is entered, there is an old stable, still standing, and through the gate near this place there was a road leading down to the canal and at the stop gates, as they were known, was the principle bathing place of the town.

'I have, when a boy, seen sometimes a score of men or boys who, after bathing, of late on a summer's evening, come up the field to go home and, when the gate was neared, a deal of silence would prevail and a closing in of ranks would take place and everyone appeared to have a desire to be first past the stable end and into the open field and little was said until Harborough Hill was reached.'

While Mr Widdop refers to the canal in his notice it should, of course, be remembered that it was not constructed until some ten years or so after Martha's dreadful deed.

Another point of interest is that the Dearne Valley appears once to have been a beauty spot – with woods and a place for bathing – before the advent of canals, railways and mining into the Dearne Rift.

Unfortunately, there appears to be no contemporaneous account of the murder and those that do exist, conflict with each other in certain areas. We know nothing of what happened to John Wild or his remaining family and indeed, are unsure as to Martha's fate. Peggie Parrington's account, however, does contain some superfluous information such as the fact that Ann Fletcher's cottage, where Martha was raised, collapsed shortly after her dark deed.

It also seems that our nude runner, Honoria Dawes, was the daughter of a lady from a renowned Yorkshire family who was disowned by them for marrying beneath her station.

Not surprisingly – in view of the alleged haunting – Martha gained a reputation as the 'Barnsley Witch'. She died on July 18th, 1795 but if you live in the Old Mill area of town, perhaps you may still be able to catch sight of her one dark night – and possibly throw some light on an event which took place over two centuries ago.

Victim: ***John Fish, shot,*** **1787**

Crowds of people stood at the bottom of Market Hill and watched local blacksmith Samuel Truelove aim his blunderbuss-type shotgun three times at Hoylandswaine rag-gatherer John Fish and three times squeeze the trigger. On the first two occasions the weapon failed to fire. Then, Mr Truelove disappeared into his nearby smithy. There he eased the lock of the firearm, inserted a new flint and augmented the charge with hob-nails. Ignoring a plea from one Edward Moore to cease his actions, the smith took aim at John Fish for a third time and shot him dead.

His body rolled from the roof of a building he was starting to demolish, and would have crashed to the ground had it not been for his clothing snagging on part of the building's structure, leaving him suspended in mid-air.

Many of the onlookers, believing their taunts against the smith had played a part in the death of the luckless Mr Fish, immediately fled the scene. But one man, by the name of Foljambe Wood, followed Truelove back to his smithy and declared: 'You old villain – do you know what you have done? 'You have taken the life of yonder poor man! I will have you bound hand and foot and taken to York Castle.'

York Castle is exactly where Samuel Truelove finished up, awaiting his trial at York Assizes. Yet so many people appeared to vouch for his good character – telling the court that he had 'shoed thousands of horses without ever pricking one' – that the jury took the remarkable course of clearing him of murder and substituting manslaughter.

Truelove was fined £20 and jailed for two years, but it seems, justice works in mysterious ways. During his incarceration he was seized by what was described as 'mortification in his feet' – so badly that his toes rotted off.

His eventual release found him unable to work again and fit only to hobble the streets of Barnsley on crutches to bear the pointed finger of scorn from adults and taunts such as: 'Shoot, shoot, you old villain', from children.

John Fish, on the other hand was immortalised, in a ballad — part of which ran:

A poor honest man, John Fish was his name.
About his own business to Barnsley he came;
But little he thought it would be his sad lot
By a bloodthirsty smith to be brutally shot.

And brutal his killing was, Fish's body was carried to the nearby Six Ringers Inn where, according to the ballad, 50 pieces of shot were found lodged in his back, 26 in his arms and 'a great number' in his head. In fact, a rustic rhymer, Robert M'Lintock, who witnessed the post mortem examination, declared that Fish's back was as 'full of shot as a Christmas pudding was full of currants'.

The date of the dastardly deed was June 26, 1787, at which time Barnsley's Moot Hall stood at the top of a group of shops and cottages in the centre of Market Hill. At the bottom end of the block, near the bridge over the River Sough (a dyke which now flows under the town), was the smithy and some dilapidated shops. It was these buildings which the town's magistrates had decided should be demolished, and upon which John Fish was working at the time of his murder. Mr Tattershall, the barber, and Mr Morton, the tinker, did not oppose their wishes, although the latter could not afford another shop and domiciled himself in the Jury Room of the Moot Hall, where he remained until half-starved, he was removed to the workhouse.

As befitting his trade however, Samuel Truelove resisted the magistrate's decision with an iron will. They therefore decided to 'unroof' his premises as a last resort.

They did, however, decide to start work on the empty shops near his home, in the hope that Truelove would accept that his position was hopeless. So it was that demolition workers started work on the shops that June day, only to be confronted by Truelove and his gun.

They didn't take long to realise they were putting their lives at risk and discontinued work. It was then that 24-year-old John Fish came on the scene and was offered a 'paltry sum' to take up where they had left off.

In John Hugh Burland's account of the matter he says that 'unfair means were adopted to screw his courage up to the sticking point' which was 'all too palpable and to be regretted'.

The same account also claims that Fish had had his fortune told by a gypsy in his youth, and been told that whatever did befall him, he wasn't born to be shot. He had also served in the army and escaped being perforated then, and so did not have too much fear of the blunderbus-wielding old smith. Like the demolition contractors however, Fish decided to start work on the adjascent shops rather than the smithy. But when Truelove arrived with his gun and his threats, he continued loosening slates with apparent unconcern. No doubt he flinched when the hammer came down on the weapon on the first occasion and even the second, but to have descended from the building would have meant losing face in front of the spectators, who were jeering and taunting the smith and his useless gun. But after Truelove's makeshift repair, the crowd was no longer laughing and Fish was in no position to.

Sad to state, Fish's elderly parents were not informed of their son's melancholy fate until some time later. They then went to his grave in St Mary's Church, where they knelt and wept.

Truelove surrendered to Honorary Constable Joseph Walker and deputy constable Richard Woodcock a short time after the killing, and was taken before Francis Edmunds, Esq., of Worsbrough Hall, who committed him to York Castle – refusing several offers of bail for Truelove, but permitting him the luxury of a feather bed mattress.

At the Assizes, Truelove was represented by Mr Richard Fenton, of Bank Top, Worsbrough, and a Mr Clarke, of Harborough House. Obviously they did well on his behalf, although Truelove is reported as thinking himself better off hanged because of the expenses incurred. Had he known that he was to become a destitute cripple, taunted by mischievous boys and sung about in ballads, he might even have asked for the rope.

Perhaps happily, in his case, he died shortly after his release at the age of 68.

BLACK BARNSLEY Profile 6

Victim: ***Thomas Parkin, shot,*** **October 1819**

Gamekeeper Thomas Parkin was blasted amidriffs by a shotgun at almost point-blank rage... his death was already assured, but with superhuman effort, he managed to ensure that the same fate did not befall his friend and colleague, Joseph Parkin. Somehow he realised that Parkin was being bludgeoned with sticks and gun butts by the three poachers they had intercepted. Further the poachers' shouts of 'Stick him, stick him', left him in no doubt that the villainous trio were intent on double murder.

Gathering his fleeting senses together, he managed to raise his gun and fire. His shot wounded one of the poachers in the shoulder. The other two ceased their murderous attack on Joseph Parkin and helped their stricken comrade run from the scene.

Joseph Parkin then hobbled from the Sheffield to Halifax turnpike road near Wharncliffe Lodge to Wortley where he lived. Thomas Parkin, his lifeblood ebbing away, managed to crawl to a nearby cottage where he died the following evening.

Although taking place on the outskirts of our area, the murder of Thomas Parkin provides an interesting chapter in our Black Barnsley series, because of the interest it created as well as the victim's heroism. A report of the crime, printed some years after its

commission, noted that crowds had flocked to see the ground of Tankersley or Wharncliffe Park steeped in blood where Thomas Parkin had fallen.

It continued: 'This tragical occurrence produced deep sensation not only in the neighbourhood where it happened but throughout the country and, perhaps tended, by some degree, to bring about the alteration of the Game Laws for which Lord Wharncliffe had long unsuccessfully contended – the legalising of the sale of game in our markets in the same manner as any other commodity.'

The background to the case was also interesting. Parkin had been a poacher himself, caught by a gamekeeper 'with no little difficulty.'

In refusing inducements to 'peach' on his accomplices when hauled before James Archibald Stuart Wortley, Parkin so impressed the lord that he was offered a position as gamekeeper. His unhappy departure from this life started on a fine sunny Sunday morning in October 1819, when he and his namesake came upon 35-year-old Samuel Booth and two 19-year-olds: W. Garrett and R. Bower.

Parkin strode up to Booth and unceremoniously passed his hand down his clothing to feel for game, guns or other poaching equipment. Feeling a gun, he attempted to seize it, at which Booth stepped back saying: 'Damn thee, art though going to rob me?'

Parkin stated: 'I must have that gun' but Booth replied: 'Thou shalt have its contents' and fired the gun into Parkin's stomach.

The same contemporary report adds that the trio then belaboured Joseph Parkin with bludgeons and gun butts, so that he received 'more thwacks on his sconce than would have been agreeable to a rhinoceros'. He fought well, parried some knocks and dealt others, but was likely to have finished up dead had it not been for Thomas Parkin managing to raise himself on one knee and fire his gun.

Parkin died shortly after being visited by Lord Wharncliffe and Archdeacon Corbett, in the knowledge that his wife and four children were to be allowed a pension of £20 a year. In fact his son, George continued in the same vocation of his hapless father and went on to become Lord Wharncliffe's head gamekeeper – a position he held for several years.

Booth, Garrett and Bower were quickly apprehended and later faced trial for the wilful murder of Thomas Parkin at the March session of York Assizes. All three were found guilty and sentenced to death, although the sentence was later remitted for Garrett and Bower. Booth met his death by hanging at the 'new drop' behind the walls of the castle at York on May 15, 1820.

Black Barnsley — Profile 7

Victim: ***Thomas Askeron, shot,*** **1829**

Thomas Askeron must be counted as one of the most unfortunate victims of violence in Barnsley. I say that because he suffered what must have been a long and painful end to his young life after receiving a gunshot wound to his knee in October 1829, and also because there was never any evidence to show that he was the intended victim. It may well be, in fact, that there was no intended victim, that the gun was discharged accidentally. But as no-one ever admitted to having fired the shot, and those who might have been able to give prosecution evidence were too frightened, no-one ever knew for certain. It seems, therefore, that Thomas Askeron must be considered the luckless victim of an industrial dispute, or to be more precise, the weavers' riots of 1829.

To examine the story fully we must first look into the events leading up to the riots and the reading of the Riot Act on the Barebones – an area of land in the New Street and Wood Street area of Barnsley which reportedly and perhaps appropriately for this collection of historic accounts, got its name from an ancient gibbet which once stood there.

The villain of the piece appears to have been cheap imports of cloth from Germany. By May 1829, Barnsley's linen merchants found their cloth virtually unsaleable in the home markets. Indeed the since closed newspaper, the *Sheffield Iris*, reported one merchant's trip down South and the presenting to him of a bill of sale for German cloth. His comments were: 'Low as wages are in Barnsley, I could not get up the same articles at the price they were purchased at.' Perhaps not surprisingly therefore, merchants throughout the country decided to reduce the rates paid to their weavers – and that caused riots in Manchester, Rochdale, Stockport, Blackburn, Burnley, Macclesfield and Spitalfields, before spreading to Barnsley.

Locally the weavers decided not to accept the reduced rates, and voiced their frustration against the warehouse owners and the handful of their own number who continued to work as blacklegs.

By early October 1829 Barnsley resembled a town under siege. The homes and warehouses of the employers were boarded up as were those of blackleg labour. Scores of special constables had been sworn in and many of them had been armed and stationed at the warehouses and the boarded-up homes. A contingent of Dragoons were also drafted into the town.

Interestingly, one of the leading blacklegs was a man by the name of Scargill – in this case William – who continued to weave by candlelight while his windows were shuttered and covered by tin sheets.

As the dispute dragged on, the weavers and their families voiced their frustration in numerous acts of public disorder. Things became so bad that the *Sheffield Mercury* commented: 'Even the women take part in the riots and the whole population is in a state of insurrection.'

On Friday, October 9th, a cart containing eight warps and guarded by constables and specials were spotted by a mob on its way to the premises of William Smith, of Wilson's Piece, near Pall Mall, at the bottom end of the Barebones. Within minutes the premises were besieged by a crowd of 500 and, at one point, a special constable by the name of Gilbanks drew his pistol, pointed it at a man by the name of John Hirst and fired. Thankfully the weapon was loaded only with powder and Mr Hirst suffered nothing worse than slight burns. Captain Slade, commander of the Dragoons, did little to quieten the mob when he refused to take Gilbanks into custody for his rash act and merely had him escorted home. The Riot Act was read to the demonstrators at 8 p.m.

Despite this, the house was still under siege at 9 p.m. the following night when Thomas Askeron, in some accounts named as 'Askron' and 'Ascham', appeared on the scene on his way home from the market.

Apparently, without warning, a pistol was discharged from the Smith's house and Askeron fell to the ground. From the outset the wound was considered dangerous, and most people agreed that young Askeron would lose his limb or his life. Unfortunately for him, it was the latter. Judging by the fact that the inquest was opened on Sunday, December 13th, it seems likely that Askeron died on Saturday the 12th – two months after the shooting.

By then the weavers had been defeated. Near starvation having forced them to break ranks, and many of the their leaders were in prison cells awaiting trial for public disorder offences.

Smith himself had been accused by the weavers of firing the shot which felled Askeron. He was arrested and taken before the magistrates, but no evidence being offered against him, he was discharged. One fact in his favour was that persons testifying against him were likely to be arrested themselves and charged for their part in the disorder, which could see them faced with three months' hard labour, and a binding over with sureties against their future good behaviour needed.

Some weavers took the law into their own hands. In the 24 hours following the shooting, 18 shots were fired into Smith's house. No-one was injured but several family members had close escapes. Shots were also fired into other houses and the wife of a Mr James Bradshaw suffered a bullet graze to her breast. A reward of £100 was offered for information leading to the arrest of those responsible for the shots.

All that could have been of little comfort to Askeron, described as 'young', although his age and occupation do not appear to have been documented. Thomas Badger presided at the inquest at the time members of the mob were still too frightened to give evidence because they would have compromised their own liberty. In these circumstances, the jury returned a verdict that Askeron, 'died from a wound in the leg suffered from a gun or pistol shot, but from whom or by whom, or how occasioned, or under what circumstances it was received, the jury had no way of ascertaining.'

By that time, another newspaper had reported that the warehouses of Barnsley were 'thronged' with 'work being given out and taken in. Looms heard going on every hand and pieces of work and other appendages are being carried in all directions.'

The weavers had lost – but Thomas Askeron had lost the most.

Victim: ***George Blackburn, clubbed to death,*** **October 1840**

The last word uttered by Worsbrough farmer George Blackburn was 'murder'... He was right, for only hours later he was dead. He had been clubbed down by a Barnsley youth – John Mitchell – who was then barely 17 years old. Despite his tender years John Mitchell must rank as Barnsley's most notorious villain ever. He confessed to having taken part in some thousand robberies – many of them cowardly and brutal – and these confessions were printed by the *Northern Star* newspaper during the month of April 1841 as a 'wholesome lesson of advice'.

The newspapers stated: 'When we tell you that this youth confesses to have been guilty of more than 1000 robberies, some accomplished with the greatest violence and with many extraordinary results, before he attained his 17th year, we may at once declare him to have left Robin Hood, Dick Turpin, Jack Shephard and all the tribe of vulgar villains far in the shade.'

The confessions, printed under Mitchell's nickname of 'Gypsy Jack' would, of course, have come as no comfort to George Blackburn, who met a particularly violent death just yards from his farmhouse home on October 5, 1840.

The farmhouse, known as Elmhirst Farm stood opposite the old sanitorium which graced the crown of Mount Vernon Road, until being demolished in recent years to make way for the Mount Vernon Hospital. The farm is still tenanted today. Remember that, at that time, the famous Upper Sheffield Road cutting had probably never been considered, and the main Barnsley to Sheffield route wound its way to Birdwell via Mount Vernon, Ward Green, Worsbrough Bridge and Worsbrough Village.

George Blackburn was a fairly well-to-do farmer with an extensive milk sales business in Barnsley. On the night in question he was making his way home on foot. At around 7 p.m. his young servant girl, Emma Fretwell, saw the heads of two men behind the stack-garth in the farmyard. She went out to see Mr Blackburn approaching up the quiet lane. He also saw the men and demanded

32 The late Worsbrough historian Mr Alfred O. Elmhirst indicates the place where George Blackburn fell. According to local folklore grass has refused to grow there ever since.

to know what they were doing there.

One replied: 'Damn thee – we'll let thee know'. Then both men leaped on the wall and Mr Blackburn was felled by a stone weighing between 10 and 12 lb. Mr Blackburn got up, staggered and fell down again. The girl rushed at the two men screaming, then turned back and ran to the house. In doing so, she spotted two other men hiding behind a water barrel before shouting to Mrs Blackburn that two men were 'murdering' her husband. When the two women ran back outside they saw two men standing over a prone Mr Blackburn. One was brandishing a gate spar measuring five feet long by about four or five inches in width. At a signal from one of the men behind the water barrel, all four men ran off. The women hurried to a sentry standing on guard at the nearby Army garrison (believed to have been at the sanitorium) and he turned out the guard.

Mr Blackburn, one eye hanging from its socket, was carried into the house, but never spoke again, and died early the following morning. His injuries included a severe fracture of the skull. Later that day saw the arrest of Gypsy Jack Mitchell at his parents' home in Shambles Street, Barnsley. Another man by the name of George Robinson was taken that evening at a Barnsley brothel.

The inquest was opened in front of Thomas Badger at Ward Green's Horse and Jockey on October 7th and adjourned until the 15th to be held at the Red Lion, Worsbrough Bridge. In the meantime 23 year old William Fox had been arrested at his mother's home. She had denied he was there, but some of his clothing was spotted and Fox, dressed only in his vest, was duly captured.

October 9 saw a large concourse of spectators outside St Mary's Church, Barnsley, for Mr Blackburn's funeral.

The following day, Mitchell was heard singing in prison. Robinson heard Mitchell and shouted to him. He received the reply: 'They've got nought against me, for when they took me before the magistrates, the girl did not know me.' Mitchell, however, faced a shock at the resumed inquest hearing on the 15th when it was revealed that his trousers had blood on them. Robinson, on the other hand, produced three witnesses to say he was in Barnsley's Wine Shades public house on the night of the offence. Fox also called witnesses to say he was in Bold Hey's beer house in Barnsley.

The hearing was again adjourned, this time to the 20th, when the Red Lion was described as 'much crowded' and the road to it from Barnsley 'lined with people'.

It took the jury eight hours to consider the evidence of the amazing number of 66 witnesses they had heard on the three days of proceedings. Then they committed Mitchell for trial as 'principal' in the wilful murder of George Blackburn, with William Fox charged with aiding and abetting. Robinson, aged 23 and a fourth man, John Cherry aged 24 were committed as accessories before the fact.

After being imprisoned in York Castle, where he made his amazing confessions, Mitchell was found guilty of murder at York Assizes and sentenced to death. The sentence was however, later commuted to one of transportation for life. All three others were acquitted.

What happened to Gypsy Jack Mitchell after the trial may never be known. But his confessions published in the *Northern Star* did reveal a lot about his early life.

He was not a true gypsy, but was one of 15 children born to a 'poor but honest' bricklayer who married twice. Indeed Mitchell's father appears to have been so good a man that on the night of the murder he prayed that the 'perpetrators' be caught before the next day was over. Mitchell appears to have been inclined to bad conduct from the start and was expelled from school.

But his real involvement with criminality started when he agreed to accompany a stranger to a public house some time before the age of twelve. Mitchell was plied with drink and awoke to find himself in a small gypsy encampment consisting of four men, four women and three other children who, Mitchell always believed, had like himself been kidnapped.

His first acts of lawlessness were confined to stealing grass from fields for the gypsy livestock. But soon he was trained to steal geese, ducks and fowl while selling pots, pans and glass. He soon learned that if he came home empty handed then he did not eat. Rustling of horses and cattle followed. Then he was trained in the robbery of lone walkers and horsemen as the gypsies plied their dishonest activites in an area ranging from 30 miles north of London to 20 miles north of York with Birmingham as their favourite hunting ground. The gypsies were always well armed with pistols but preferred to use knives, bayonets or staves to subdue their victims when necessary. They would, however, use all weapons at their disposal, particularly if their camp site was attacked.

Mitchell claimed he did not 'know to having killed anyone specifically,' but suspected that some of his victims might have died from their injuries.

He was still facing the death sentence when he admitted he struck Mr Blackburn with the gate spar. He accused his acquitted colleague Robinson of throwing the stone which felled Mr Blackburn and

Cherry of being with them.

Premeditated and savage, the murder of George Blackburn shocked the people of Barnsley so much so that one or two people chronicled the event in verse. One such person was John Hugh Burland, on whose writings many of our *Black Barnsley* profiles have relied. His poem is as follows:

His limbs were bound in the lonesome cell,
With black remorse in his heart to dwell,
That one so young could do such a deed,
As life to take for unlawful greed,
It's indeed most sad to the upright mind,
As it shows how base may become mankind.

Near Vernon's Mount is the blood-stained land,
Where Blackburn fell by the ruffian's hand,
The place is known as the Elmhirst Farm,
'Twas there he dwelt with no thought of harm,
But he was waylaid near his own door stone,
And with fatal stroke he was made to moan.

A stone was hurled with a fearful bound,
Which laid him low on the damp, cold ground,
His servant screamed for she saw him fall,
The wretches fled over the planting wall,
From the barracks near sped some soldiers brave,
But they were too tardy, his life to save.

Stern justice reached the worst of the gang,
Who dealt the blow which gave the death pang,
His brow was sear'd with foul murder's brand,
And he was sent to a penal land,
Like many beast of prey to be barr'd and chained,
In thrall to be held where his life remained.

The poem, apart from its dubious literary merits, tells us little about the crime that we do not know apart from the third line of the last verse: 'His brow was sear'd with foul murder's brand' – this seems to imply that the practice of branding a 'C' on the forehead of killers to denote Caine's murder of his brother, Abel, was still in use in the 1840s.

Victim: *Henry Walker, shot,* January 1841

William Clarke, alias 'Slenderman' always denied pulling the trigger of the gun which killed gamekeeper Henry Walker. Even when the grand jury at Lincoln Assizes took just 30 minutes to find him guilty of wilful murder, he stated: 'I am not guilty – I did not fire the shot.' But when the time came for his execution, he did appear penitent. Writers of the time noted that he walked 'with a firm step' in the procession from his condemned cell to the gallows in the yard of Lincoln Castle and mounted the scaffold without assistance.

But as he stood moments away from death he cried out: 'May the Lord have mercy on me' several times and had said the first two words of that final petition for mercy once more, when the bolt was drawn and he plunged to his death.

Whether those words meant that he actually admitted murder rather than being just a party to it, the public of Barnsley never knew. They were rather more concerned with the question of whether 44-year-old Slenderman was really a Barnsley man at all.

Burland perhaps summed up the feelings of the township, when he wrote:

'Taking previous habit and repute into account, the announcement of the execution of William Clarke, alias Slenderman, at Lincoln on Monday last, for murder under circumstances of peculiar aggravation, would give a rude shock to one of our most cherished traditions.

'Clarke was described as a Barnsley man and so he was, in the sense of having lived and worked in the town some years ago, yet he wasn't a Barnsley man in the proper acceptance of the term, i.e. he was not a native and he did not commit the crime for which he suffered death by hanging while an inhabitant of Barnsley.

'It will therefore be seen that our good name is only slightly, if at all tarnished and we trust the day is far distant when Barnsley will furnish a bona fide Barnsley subject for the gallows.'

In fact, Clarke's contention that he had not fired the shot which robbed Henry Walker of his life, could have been true. His accomplices in the poaching expedition that went wrong may have been able to concoct a story that would make his part in the affair blacker than it actually was. They certainly turned Queen's evidence against him.

The story started on January 30, 1841 when Clarke, a bricklayer who had worked on the construction of Barnsley's Old Mill gasworks, set off to poach in woods at Norton Disney near Newark in the company of George Garner (30), William Fletcher (27) and George Wood (30).

Also abroad in Eagle Wood that night were Mr Walker, head gamekeeper for Mr Charles Graham, of Crawford, Middlesex, and two colleagues named as Wells and Lynn. On reaching the wood, the poachers split into two parties with Clarke and Garner together.

Some time later the noise of gunfire acquainted the gamekeeper of the poachers' presence. Lynn was sent for assistance while Walker and Wells went to investigate. They encountered Clarke and Garner. A chase ensued until Clarke turned, dropped onto one knee, levelled his gun and shouted: 'Stand back or else I'll blow your brains out.' Walker replied, 'I'll not stand back.'

A further chase ensued ending with another confrontation during which Walker announced:

'If you'll put that gun down and stand, we'll fight like men.'

Again Clarke and Garner continued their flight with the keeper in hot pursuit. Then Clarke is said to have dropped to one knee, turned and fired. Walker fell with a wound to his knee, exclaiming: 'Lord have mercy upon me – I'm shot.' He died one week later.

Garner, Fletcher and Wood, all local men were apprehended on the following day. Clarke was arrested nearly three weeks later, a reward of £50 for his capture – a tidy sum in those days – having been offered. He was apprehended by Superintendent Brown of the Lincolnshire Constabulary, in a public house at Lowestoft while waiting to sail for Ireland as second hand on a mackerel fishing smack.

As stated, Clarke was found guilty at the end of the Lincoln Assizes hearing. The case against Fletcher and Wood was thrown out by the grand jury. Garner, the only man actually with Clarke and the first to turn Queen's evidence, had no evidence offered against him and was able to return to his life as a free man.

Clarke maintained the same stolid demeanour as he had done throughout the trial, when sentenced to death by Mr Justice Denman. He steadfastly claimed that he had not fired the fatal shot which robbed a brave gamekeeper of his life.

He always maintained that his partners in crime had conspired against him. That could well have been the case. With the benefit of hindsight, it would appear that the most reliable information offered to the court would have been from Walker's colleague, Wells. Unfortunately his evidence has not been documented.

Why Clarke was known as Slenderman is not clear either, although it is known that he used several aliases. One titbit of information that was recorded about him was the fact that he weighed 13 stone – not that slender for those times!

Victim: ***William Huntley, clubbed, June 1830, discovered* 1664**

In mid-1841, Police Constable Gernon travelled from the Vale of Cleveland to Barnsley with a grisly cargo in his bag. He was looking for Robert Goldsborough and he found him. Arriving at Goldsborough's home, P.C. Gernon reached into his bag and produced from it a human skull. He placed it on the table in front of Goldsborough and coolly asked him if he thought it bore any resemblance to William Huntley. Perhaps, not surprisingly, 47-year-old Goldsborough appeared agitated; and it was only after a considerable pause and with tears in his eyes that he was able to say he knew nothing about it. Days later he was en route to Stokesley, where evidence was heard against him prior to his committal to York Assizes.

In the end, Goldsborough was acquitted of the murder of William Huntley – but not before another man died. And that makes for an interesting story in our Black Barnsley profiles, despite the fact that the murder of which Goldsborough was accused, if indeed it was murder, took place many miles away from Barnsley.

The strange case of Robert Goldsborough could have been lost from our series had it not been for the services of the *Northern Star* and Sunderland-based *Northern Times* newspapers.

Their issues of August 18th, 1842, describe how the whole Vale of Cleveland and Hutton Rudby in particular was in 'great excitement' in June of 1830, when William Huntley mysteriously disappeared.

Huntley, known to have kept company with poachers, and was also known to have been in possession of a considerable sum of money. On the night of his disappearance, Huntley had been seen in the company of Robert Goldsborough and a man by the name of George Garbutt. Everyone suspected that Huntley had been murdered by those two men but the body was never found.

Goldsborough's home was searched and Huntley's watch and several other items of his were found – including a quantity of banknotes. Goldsborough explained by saying that the items were

part payment of a debt owed to him by Huntley who, he said, had set off for America. Unable to prove otherwise, the authorities appear to have accepted Goldsborough's account. Certainly, he was never charged with any serious felony and, some time later, he left the North Riding for the West Riding of Yorkshire, where he is said to have assumed another name.

Garbutt, having robbed a barn, was also obliged to leave the area, though, some time later, was reported to be working in Sunderland as a coal-trimmer.

It was not until June 1841, that interest in Huntley's disappearance was reawakened. It was then that workmen were engaged in cutting a new course for a rivulet running through Stokesley in the direction of Hutton Rudby to make a straighter course for Tame Bridge. In the old water course they came across a quantity of bones. At first they thought they belonged to an unlucky cow – until they uncovered a human skull. A doctor by the name of Stother told a later inquest that the deceased had received a blow to the back of the head and a jury returned a verdict of 'death by foul means' – hence P.C. Gernon's excursion to Barnsley.

It was during the preliminary hearing in Stokesley that the first really damning evidence against Goldsborough was given by one Thomas Grundy. He told the hearing that he had been knocked up at his home by Goldsborough on the night of Huntley's disappearance and taken to a wood where Goldsborough told him he wanted him to carry a 'bundle' into Stokesley. Inside the bundle he found a man's head, became frightened and asked Goldsborough what he had been doing. It took Goldsborough five minutes to answer. He said that he had shot Huntley by accident, and added that he would shoot Grundy if he told anyone about it. Grundy told the court he managed to escape from Goldsborough, but was afraid to go out until after Goldsborough left the area.

Goldsborough, in his defence, still maintained that Huntley had given him the proceeds from the sale of his loom, shook hands with him and set off for America.

Both Goldsborough and Grundy were committed for trial at York Assizes, but Grundy never appeared in the dock. His body was found suspended by the neck in York Castle prison, an end officially attributed to suicide.

Perhaps, not surprisingly – in the absence of evidence from Grundy – the evidence against Goldsborough was described as 'purely circumstantial' and he was discharged on March 2nd, 1842.

Whether or not Goldsborough returned to Barnsley is not known. However, it is known that in the autumn of 1830 – shortly after Huntley's disappearance – Goldsborough arrived in the town and took a room at the home of William Robinson, from whom he also rented a room, in Kingstone Place. Accounts have it that he remained there for a month and then left. It was some time later that he returned carrying not one but two watches apparently once owned by Huntley, and also some of his clothing. It is also known that he unsuccessfully attempted to sell one of the watches to a watchman by the name of William White, who lived in Cordeux Row.

Looking back on the affair after a century-and-a-half, it must be said that Grundy's untimely departure from the world, apparently by his own hand, was certainly fortuitous for Goldsborough. Was it really a case of felo-de-se, or was it that someone was trying to conceal something more sinister?

And what happened to Garbutt – the man who could be termed the missing link in the strange case of William Huntley? We will never know. Our forefathers certainly didn't. As the saying goes: 'Dead men tell no tales' — even when the back of the skull is caved in from the blast of a gun.

Victim: ***Thomas Depledge, clubbed,*** **October 1841**

Thomas Depledge met a savage death on October 11, 1841, and must rank as Barnsley's most unfortunate murder victim. For the 21-year-old farm servant was the victim of a case of mistaken identity. When Wombwell brothers William and Joseph Lodge struck him down one dark night at Darfield crossroads, they thought they were getting even with one of two men with whom they had quarrelled and skirmished earlier that night. In fact, Depledge had met the two men in question and walked some way in their company, but he had not been with them when they had encountered the Lodge brothers earlier.

The local populace felt so sorry about Depledge's innocent departure from this life that, by public subscription, they erected a commemorative stone on a site near the murder spot. On that stone was the following inscription:

'To the memory of Thomas Depledge who lost his life,
October 11th 1841.
At midnight dread by this wayside,
A murdered man, poor Depledge died.
The guiltless victim of a blow
Designed to lay another low,
From men whom he had never harmed
By hate and drunken passion warmed.
Hence learn to shun in youth's fresh spring
The courses which to ruin bring.'

In fact the stone did not remain there long as relatives decided to place it on Depledge's grave in Clayton churchyard. The vicar there objected to the inscription and it was replaced by: 'In memory of Thomas Depledge, aged 21, cruelly murdered on the Highway near Darfield. October 11th 1841.'

The events leading up to the vicious murder appear to have started when the Lodge brothers, both boat haulers, met up with two other men at Measbrough Dyke while returning to Wombwell from Barnsley Fair. Accounts of that meeting differ. That chronicled in *Lodge's Almanack 1904-7* names the other two men as Milnes and Marsden and says they overtook the Lodges. The account printed in Wilkinson's history, however, names the men as Mills and Marsden and says that they were on foot and the Lodges on horseback. Obviously, in that account, it was the riders who overhauled the walkers. Both do agree, however, that the two parties quarrelled, and the Wilkinson account says Joseph Lodge dismounted and bit one of the men 'severely' on the cheek and almost bit two fingers off the other. Despite that, it was the Lodges who appear to have lost the fight. Battered and bruised and with one having lost his hat, they returned to Barnsley to collect a posse of friends to help even the score.

Mills and Marsden, in the meantime, must have set off again at a cracking pace for they had reached Darfield's Ring o' Bells public house before their next encounter with the Lodges. By that time, the Lodge posse had virtually disbanded with most members opting to go home after several fruitless searches of public houses. The brothers' nephew, John Lodge, was still with them, however, when they entered the Ring o' Bells and found Mills, Marsden and their missing hat. The encounter in the pub stopped short of violence, but was unpleasant enough for those within to entreat Mills and Marsden not to continue their journey to Billingley after the Lodges left. Ironically, its possible that one of those advising them to stay the night there may have been young Thomas Depledge, who is said to have resembled Mills closely in both appearances and dress.

Despite the possibility of finding the Lodges waiting for them outside, Mills and Marsden left the back kitchen of the Ring o' Bells to walk home with a group of other men including Depledge. Unfortunately, they did not all walk at the same pace and became separated. Mills and Marsden were at the front with Depledge close behind and the others still further back.

Those others were soon overtaken by Joseph and William Lodge their nephew having been left at Darfield bridge. The brothers were now on foot, and one was carrying a hedgestake.

Soon after that the rearmost walkers came upon the lifeless form of Thomas Depledge. He was weltering in his own blood, his nose was completely flattened and he had died almost immediately.

The party, who carried the hapless Depledge to a nearby house, didn't see the Lodge brothers again that night. Ironically, the intended victims did. Mills and Marsden were still walking home, unaware that they had escaped a bloody reckoning intended for them, when they were overtaken by the fleeing brothers. The latter turned down a lane to Wombwell where they were arrested later the same night.

Both brothers were found guilty of murder at York Assizes in March 1842 and were ordered to be transported for 15 years. John Lodge, who lived at Goldthorpe, was acquitted.

At first sight the departure of young Thomas Depledge is a simple if tragic murder lacking in mystery it not misfortune. But the fact that the commemorative stone was bought by public subscription shows the interest that was shown in the affair at the time.

There are points which are not clarified by either account, such as whether the two warring factions were known to each other before their meeting at Measbrough Dyke, and why was Depledge not able to tell the brothers of the mistake they were making? His nose injury seems to indicate he had time to turn and confront the Lodges, rather than being cruelly felled from behind. Perhaps most intriguing is the question: 'When did the Lodge brothers realise their mistake? Was it after they had attacked Depledge, or when they ran past Mills and Marsden or, indeed, after their arrest? We will never know.

All we do know is that Thomas Depledge must be considered one of life's most unfortunate victims

Thomas Depledge's Tombstone at All Saints' Church, Frickley and Clayton. On the tombstone, still clearly visible today and unusual by the words 'was cruelly murdered'.

Victim: ***George Firth, shot,*** **January 1851**

Few murder victims have gone to their grave not knowing who their assassin was, but that appears to have been the case with George Firth back in January 1851. And if George Firth did not know who callously pointed a gun at the back of his head and sent a ball spinning into his brain, it's not surprising that no one else found out either. To this day, George Firth's departure from life remains a baffling mystery, particularly as the crime appears to have been well thought out, well executed and, perhaps, motiveless.

Interest in the case was intense from the start, and grew when the victim's brother, John Firth, was charged with murder and tried at York Assizes. So much so that the lengthy court proceedings were held up for some time when the princely sum of £50 was offered 'for anyone who should give such information as would lead to the conviction of the murderer'. The offer of the reward was even accompanied by the promise of a free pardon to any accomplice in the crime as long as he was not the actual perpetrator. The reward was never paid. John Firth, who had protested his innocence from the start, was eventually acquitted and as far as is known, neither he nor anyone else ever confessed to the cowardly assassination.

The story of the murder of George Firth starts on the night of January 23rd when the 43-year-old coal merchant was making his way home to the small hamlet of Partridge Dale, which nestled in a valley between Silkstone Common and Thurgoland. He was climbing some steps to cross a field just 200 yards away from his home when the countryside echoed to the sound of a gun being fired. In modern language, George Firth had been 'wasted'. He died a few hours later, after telling his mother: 'It's a sad job,' and praying.

For the evidence against his brother John Firth, we must rely on that given to the coroner's inquiry, which lasted three days. That evidence included the fact that John Firth was the owner of a stick gun, kept in the cellar of his mother's home. The gun was out of repair until shortly before the tragedy, when it was sent to Silkstone for repair. John Firth was actually seen in the blacksmith's shop at

Victoria Colliery filing a portion of his walking-stick gun and making some sheet lead like a wad to fit into the end of the barrel.

John Hayes, a Silkstone Blacksmith, told the hearing he repaired a gun for John Firth at the end of November. The gun could be used for either ball or shot. And William Simpson, the blacksmith at Victoria Colliery, said that John Firth went to him and asked him to make about one-and-a-half-dozen lead balls – about half of which he took away with him the same day. Simpson also claimed that John Firth visited him shortly after the murder, took him to the corner of the house, and asked him if he had the balls yet, before adding: 'I had better get shut of them as they might get me into a hobble.'

The coroner, after lengthy summing up, cautioned John Firth, who admitted that the gun was sent for repair but he claimed it was still of no use and he had never shot with it since its return. The jury returned a verdict of 'wilful murder by some person or persons unknown'.

They added: 'We think there is much evidence to throw considerable suspicion on the brother, John Firth, but that there is not enough to warrant us coming to a verdict against him.'

After their verdict, however, John Firth was taken into custody by Superintendent Green. Firth was later alleged to have told a constable by the name of William White: 'I don't understand being apprehended again after the coroner has discharged me. I should think they cannot hang me now, whatever evidence they bring against me. If I should be transported, I should like to settle my affairs with my parents. If I am sent away for a number of years and have a chance of coming back, I should not like to have to depend upon working for my living.'

Throughout his trial at York, John Firth maintained he had not seen his brother that night, although some evidence had been given that the two men were together at the Gate Inn, Dodworth, before leaving for their homes.

Even with the benefit of hindsight, the prosecution case against John Firth must be regarded as flimsy. Nowhere, for instance, in any of the accounts is there any suggestion that there was bad blood between the brothers. Neither is there any evidence for us to presume that John Firth would have benefitted financially or otherwise from his brother's death.

The mystery is of course: If John Firth didn't kill his brother, who did? Indeed, who had any motive for such an evil crime which seems to indicate that someone lay in wait for George Firth and was well aware of his movements?

Had the crime taken place in the present day, things might have been very different. But our forefathers did not have the benefit of forensic scientists, along with the equipment, which might have been able to establish whether or not the piece of lead had been fired from the accused's gun.

One may contemplate, however, whether a cursory examination of John Firth's walking-stick gun could have established if it had been fired recently. Unfortunately, all the accounts available contain no mention of such an examination being carried out. One can only conjecture over the likelihood of a blacksmith returning a firearm still in an unusuable condition, as John Firth claimed that he did.

The author on the style where George Firth met his death. The roofs of Partridge Dale cottages can be seen on the horizon.

Victim: ***Emily Smith, throat slit,*** **March 1852**

Early on the morning of March 24, 1852, a youth by the name of Atkinson chanced upon one of the grisliest scenes ever seen in Barnsley. There before him, on land off Old Slip Inn Lane – now Carlton Road – were two bodies in a pool of blood. One belonged to a 20-year-old woman, the other to her 11-month-old daughter. Both had had their throats cut. The finding of the bodies horrified the public of Barnsley. They referred to it for years after as 'The Smithies Tragedy', rather than using the name of Annis Smith and her baby Emily.

The death of the two also mystified them. There was evidence to suggest that Annis Smith killed little Emily with a razor before turning the blade on herself, however, there was also evidence to suggest that they might have been the victim of one of the town's grisliest murders. In the end, a coroner's jury was unable to determine which was the case; nor has anyone else in later years.

The heartrending tale of the unhappy Annis Smith and her short-lived baby remains a mystery to this day, and is perhaps still best remembered as 'a tragedy'. The daughter of Joseph Laycock, Annis took the name of Smith on her marriage. But at the time of her death she had been co-habiting with a man by the name of James Gledhill for 12 months, having found out that her marriage to Smith was bigamous. Unfortunately, her association with Gledhill wasn't a happy one. On the Monday night, prior to the finding of the bodies on the Wednesday morning, the couple had had a bitter argument and Gledhill, by his own admission, had given Annis 'a good hiding'.

The latter was so bitter about the argument that she later told a neighbour that she would cut her own throat, and the child's too, and that 'James will be in York before Saturday'. That statement, coupled with the evidence of the physician who examined the bodies, should have been enough to convince our forefathers that the deaths were infanticide and suicide respectively, had it not been for the fact that Gledhill seemed to have more than his fair share of blood about his person and his home when visited by

Superintendent Green.

The sight which met the eyes of the youth, Atkinson, also seemed to cast doubt on the suicide theory, despite the fact Annice was found with a razor in her hand. She was found lying on her left side with her face to the ground and with the legs of the child on her left hand. The razor was in her right hand, but there were also marks on the ground as if, in the agony of death, she had scratched with her hands. She was also mutilated in a shocking manner with five wounds to her throat. Three were regarded by surgeon Thomas Wainwright as superficial, but the fourth was deep and the fifth was described as a 'deep gash'. In fact, neither the carotid artery or the jugular vein had been severed, which indicated that she had lived for some time before her life's blood ebbed away.

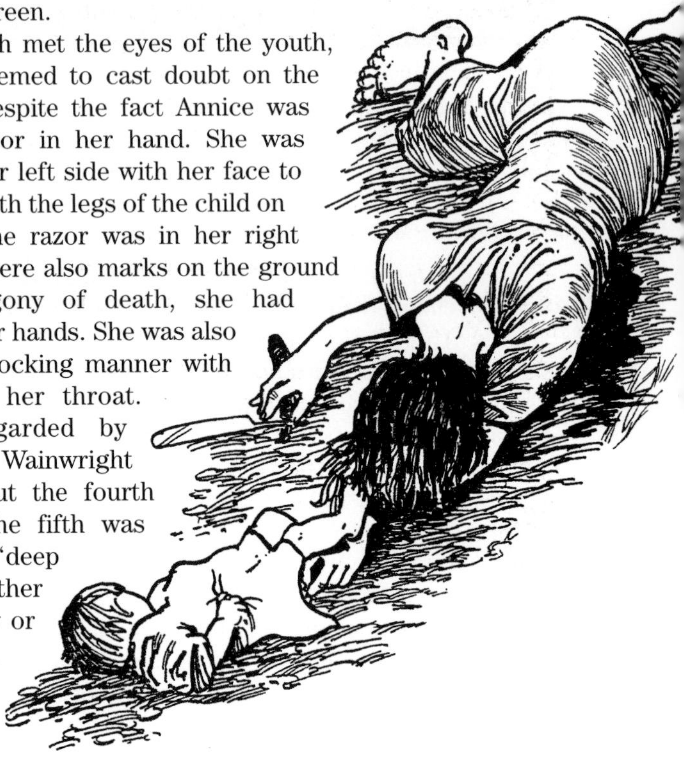

Mr Wainwright told the inquest that there was nothing about the wounds to show that they could not have been self-inflicted, but added that he could not account for the position in which they were found or the position of the razor.

In his evidence to the inquest, held at Wakefield Road's Woodman Inn where the bodies were first taken, Supt Green described how he found blood on the steps of an outhouse at Gledhill's home, how there was a large clot of blood near the chamber steps and smaller drops of blood on the house floor. There were also drops of blood about four feet from the top of the stairs, a blood spot on the bed sheets and the blanket and an empty razor case under the mattress.

There were also spots of blood on the shirt that Gledhill was wearing and on another shirt, although Gledhill explained the first of those by saying he had had a fight with a man called Thickett and the second by helping friends to kill a pig. Both of these stories were corroborated. Thickett, in fact, had fought with Gledhill after intervening in an attack by Gledhill on his common-law wife.

When summing up the evidence, the coroner told the jury they must consider whether the act was perpetrated in Carlton Lane or whether the bodies had been removed there.

If they thought there wasn't sufficient satisfactory evidence to find Gledhill, who steadfastly maintained his innocence, guilty of murder, and had some doubts about whether he did commit the deed, they were to give those doubts their consideration and give the weight of them in favour of the prisoner.

The jury returned the following verdict: 'We find that the deceased, Annis Smith, and her child found early on Wednesday morning March 24th in Carlton Lane with their throats cut and quite dead, but by whom the deed was committed, there is not evidence to show.'

BLACK BARNSLEY — Profile 14

Victim: ***Thomas Husband, broken neck,*** **December 1853**

Thomas Husband could have been garrotted and robbed on Christmas Day 1853. Similarly, he could have been the victim of an equine hit-and-run accident. The public of Barnsley never found out, and for years afterwards the incident was always described as 'the mysterious death of Thomas Husband'. Coming within two years of the equally mysterious death of Annie Smith and her baby daughter, Emily, Thomas Husband's death was bound to cause widespread interest. But the fact that he could have been attacked by robbers and garrotted, plus the fact that the 39-year-old colliery labourer from Silkstone died on Christmas night, completely captivated the public's attention.

From the outset the facts were intriguing. Husband's body was found on the highway near what used to be the old toll bar at Hoyle Mill, close to the Old Oak Well. His neck was dislocated and one of his pockets was turned inside out. There was also a snuff-like powder found in his mouth and a large mark on his back.

That mark on his back and the dislocated neck prompted chronicler/historian John Hugh Burland to write many years after the event: 'It was generally believed that the poor fellow had been seized by the arms from behind and a knee thrust into the centre of his back and that his head was pulled back and his neck broken.'

Those who believed that, may have been right, but there was also another theory put to one of the inquest sittings. That was that Husband could have been knocked down by a bus which ran from the Kings Head Hotel, Market Hill, Barnsley, to Cudworth Railway Station. That supposition was put to the driver of the bus, but he declared that his horses had shied at a dark object lying in the road, which turned out to be the body.

Facts appeared to be in remarkably short supply for the coroner's jury. What they did know was that Husband had kept the company of several bad characters – all male and all without anything to directly link them with his death.

He had spent Christmas Day drinking at various public houses in

Barnsley, and had been ejected from one for using bad language. No one, it seemed, knew when Husband decided to head for the road, nor with whom. Nor did they know why he was in Hoyle Mill.

The coroner, in his summing up, said there could scarcely be any doubt of the deceased having died from an injury to his chest, but whether he had received the injury from accident or design, was not shown by the evidence. 'You may be considering that some foul play has been at work and that it has been done for the purpose of robbing him,' added the coroner, 'as some witnesses have insinuated.' But with respect to that, the evidence was very weak and the verdict must be accordingly.'

Perhaps not surprisingly the jury returned a verdict that Thomas Husband was 'found dead' adding 'there is not sufficient evidence to show how he came to his death.'

Victim: ***Luke and Elizabeth White, clubbed,*** **December 1856**

Lay preacher Luke White was writing his Sunday sermon when a knock at the door summoned him into his chemist's shop on the night of December 4, 1856. Seconds later he was dead. He suffered blows to his head so severe that fragments of skull were pushed into his brain. Unfortunately, the noise of the attack attracted the attention of his 58-year-old wife, Elizabeth, who, candlestick in hand, walked straight to her equally violent and gruesome death.

The ferocity of the murder of Mr White, a 62-year-old chemist, druggist, postmaster, assistant overseer, vestry clerk and local Calvinistic Independent preacher, and his wife was such that it attracted attention far and beyond their home township of Bolton-on-Dearne. People were outraged that such pillars of respectability could be so brutally slaughtered in the confines of their own home.

The Home Secretary was contacted and a reward offered; and Colonel Cobbe, newly-appointed Chief Constable of the West Riding Constabulary, Superintendent Green of Barnsley and Superintendent Astwood of Doncaster all gave the case their undivided attention. Despite that, no one was ever brought to justice. The grisly double murder, which led to one of the biggest manhunts seen in the North during the 19th century, remains unsolved to this day.

Now, as then, it seems likely that the murderer or murderers were not only native to Bolton but known to Mr and Mrs White. Why else were blows still aimed at their skulls when the first blows must have rendered them insensible, if indeed not killed them? And why should Mr White have chosen to admit someone to his shop after 10 p.m. on that dark December night? Plunder was believed to have been the object of crime but very little, if anything, was taken. The police believe that the culprit or culprits took fright when the couple's dog appeared on the scene. The dog was still at the side of his fallen master when Mrs Charlotte Browning arrived at the shop the following morning, to find the shutters closed but the door open. Through an opening in the counter she was shocked to see Mr White's head lying in a pool of blood. The discovery of Mrs White's body, still dressed in her clothes of the previous day, was made by a draper, who responded to Mrs Browning's cries of alarm and entered the premises. The draper, a Mr Day, described the sight as 'sickening'. The faces of Mr and Mrs White were smeared with streaks of blood and dirt, which contrasted with their pallid countenances to give them a ghastly appearance. The fractures to their skulls had completely destroyed the contours of their heads.

The inquest was held at the appropriately-named Cross Daggers Inn, Bolton, where Dr Burman of Wath gave the gory details of the injuries suffered. At that time the principal suspect was a pot hawker by the name of William Bee, who was well known in Bolton and was apprehended on suspicion. The main evidence against him was that his shirt and jacket were stained with blood, but Bee resolutely denied any involvement in the murders and explained the blood by saying he had been on a rabbiting expedition.

Suspicion then fell on a man called William White who had unofficially acted as Parish Constable for Bolton on Dearne. Just why suspicion fell on Mr White is not made clear in John Hugh Burland's account, written many years after the murders. Indeed, he said that Mr White was present at a meeting on the night previous to the murders, at which it was decided to present a memorandum to Colonel Cobbe urging him to appoint William White as constable.

Far from being appointed constable, White was later summoned to appear before a Doncaster court on a charge of assaulting one Edward Auty. White admitted the offence but explained that Auty had insulted him, by saying the authorities wanted to know where he was on the night of the murder.

White ultimately moved from Bolton-on-Dearne to Barnsley, where he died while living in Union Row. Rumours were rife that he made a confession to the murders, but he never did. The whys, hows and wherefores of Mr and Mrs White's deaths remain unanswered, just as the Sunday sermon was never finished.

BLACK BARNSLEY — Profile 16

Victim: ***Isaac Wood, shot,*** **1858**

Young Isaac Wood thought he had won twelve quarts of ale when he played skittles with William Haigh – but in fact it had lost him his life. Twenty-four year-old Haigh apparently took umbrage at losing to the 19-year-old blast furnace filler on that fateful day of October 12th 1858. He griped at buying the beer even when Wood said he would settle for just two more quarts. And when their respective dogs decided to take a dislike to each other, the scene was set for a bloody confrontation.

The violence started just outside the Rock beerhouse in Stubbin Lane, Elsecar when Haigh threw a punch at Wood. The bachelor retaliated and punch followed punch even when the duo fell to the floor. By the time they were parted, it was evident that Haigh, described as tipsy and fresh by witnesses, had come off the worst. He was bleeding heavily from the mouth.

Peter Edwards, a Jump man, colleague of Wood's at Mr Dawes' Milton Iron Works and who also knew Haigh, tried to act as a peacemaker. He told Haigh he was too tipsy to fight and that he should go home and quieten down. Haigh seemed to respond, shaking his hand and saying, 'You and me are good friends and always were'.

But Haigh, as he departed the scene, turned and shouted, 'I will fetch something that will do for the b......'.

Wood, meanwhile, had set off for his lodgings at Nether Field, Stubbin Lane. With him was his landlady, Mrs Ellen Kidger, lodge-mate James Bell and a group of men and women. It was one of the women who first screamed a warning of Haigh's return.

He came running from his nearby home and had with him a loaded shotgun.

Friendship flew out of the window as Edwards went to intercept Haigh. He was felled when Haigh swung the gun at him, its muzzle almost cutting through his upper lip. Haigh then ran forward and levelled the shotgun at Wood, no one else tried to intervene. Wood, the son of a Leicestershire frame knitter, and although Edwards got up from the ground and made a last desperate attempt to seize the gun, he was too late. Haigh fired the shotgun at point-blank range virtually shattering the arm Wood had raised to protect his face, while other shot blasted into his head, shoulders and face with such force, that teeth were knocked out and the unfortunate teenager fell to the ground gravely injured.

Accounts of what happened then varied from witness to witness. Some said Haigh continued his brutal attack on Wood while he was on the ground, others that he once more struck the hapless Edwards with the gun.

Joseph Simms, a Hoyland carter, gave the rather unlikely version that Wood got to his feet and struck Haigh with his one good arm.

It is known, however, that Wood's lodge mate James Bell was the one to finally disarm Haigh who then ran off to his home. Wood was loaded onto a cart and first taken to his lodgings and subsequently to Sheffield Infirmary, where within hours, he was undergoing an operation to amputate his shattered left arm.

Meanwhile, Haigh had been arrested and taken to Barnsley by Parochial Constable W. Hale, who had gone to Haigh's home in company with Bell and found him lying across the hearth. Haigh offered no resistance to his arrest.

Haigh appeared in court at Barnsley the following day and was

Stubbin Lane, now Hill Street, Elsecar, in late Victorian times.

duly remanded in custody. By then, rumours were already circulating that Wood had died. In fact Wood, who had remained conscious and even given an account of events to the police before the operation, appeared to be recovering.

Four weeks after the shooting, Wood gave a deposition to Barnsley Magistrates' Clerk Thomas Marshall, in the presence of magistrates, Vincent Corbett Esq., the Hon. F. Stuart Wortley, of the famous Wharncliffe family and Haigh who was in attendance with a police escort. Wood told them that he had never seen Haigh until the day of the attack and he had only gone to the Rock, to persuade Bell to accompany him home to sleep, so they would both be refreshed for the nightshift at the ironworks.

Unfortunately, Bell was engrossed in dominoes so he went outside and played a game of ninepins with an old man who, coincidentally, was also called William Haigh and won a quart of ale from him. Wood had subsequently been reluctant to play the younger Haigh, at ninepins, preferring to get home and have a good afternoon's sleep, but he eventually relented.

Wood closed his deposition saying, 'I have been very bad the last two days but am much better now', nonetheless, three days later he was dead.

The inquest opened on Tuesday, November 14 at Sheffield Infirmary before the Coroner, Mr. Badger. Haigh was present and described as being deeply affected when the surgeon, Mr. Jonathan Barber, said he had high hopes of Wood's recovery, until a few days before his death. A post mortem had revealed that Wood had 'pus' in his blood – presumably a form of blood poisoning cause by the lead shot. The hearing concluded with the jury returning a unanimous verdict of unlawful murder against Haigh, who was committed for trial on a coroner's warrant.

Haigh eventually stood trial at York Crown Court, as a member of the Yorkshire Winter Gaol Delivery, in mid December.

According to the *Barnsley Record* newspaper, the Grand Jury, formed in the main of local gentry, ignored the bill preferred for murder and found for a true bill for manslaughter. Perhaps not surprisingly, Haigh pleaded guilty to that lesser offence. Sentencing him to four years penal servitude, Mr. Baron Watson, presiding, said he had anticipated the Grand Jury throwing out the bill of murder.

No prosecution evidence was given at that hearing.

The case of Haigh perhaps deserves special attention, because it was the first murder case to be reported by the *Barnsley Chronicle*. Although only the *Barnsley Record* is quoted in this summary, the

Chronicle reported the offence in its very first issue of October 16th 1858, and followed the case to its conclusion. The Chronicle's coverage of the inquest hearing, it is fair to say, was far better than that of the Record, which was first published in 1854.

However, neither paper felt moved to comment on Haigh's sentencing or the Grand Jury's decision to throw out the murder charge.

One might think Wood's death had to be murder. Haigh had refused to calm down, shouted a threat and then ran the 100 yards to his home before returning with a loaded weapon, with which he felled a friend who tried to disarm him, before pointing the gun at his dumbstruck victim and firing from close range. If that did not demonstrate malice aforethought, one wonders what could... though some would argue that there was a degree of mitigation by virtue of the fact that Haigh was under the influence of drink and angry at having lost money to Wood. The fact that death took place more than a month after the shooting was, no doubt, also a factor in the subsequent deliberation of the jury. Despite the fact that Wood must have suffered an agonising departure from this life.

The Grand Jury's decision is perhaps most interesting when compared to the treatment of one Richardson, 30 years later in 1888. The difference being that Richardson's victim, was a foreman at his place of work rather than simply a public house drinker.

This must raise the question as to whether Britain's judiciary in Victorian times, was mindful of the need to control the working masses at their place of work, while being much less interested in what damage they did to each other during their leisure time.

Victim: ***John Lincoln, beaten*** **April 1862**

On Saturday, May 3, 1862, the *Barnsley Chronicle* produced a special two-column supplement covering the inquest hearing on the death of little John William Lincoln. Supplements in those days were not as rare as they are now, but the fact that it was produced, gives some indication of how abhorred our former townsfolk were by the crime of infanticide.

The interest in the case was threefold: first John William was just four years old; secondly, he suffered from rickets and had never managed to walk under his own steam; thirdly, the crime was committed by his new stepmother. To be fair to the latter, 24 year old Mary Ann Lincoln, I should add that she never admitted the crime. Her version was that John William's eight year old brother, George Henry Lincoln, had allowed the hapless little mite to fall down the stairs of their home. Unfortunately for her, the jury at the Barnsley inquest did not believe her, nor did the jury at the Summer Assizes, held in July 1862 at York.

The latter's verdict that Mary Ann Lincoln was guilty as charged of manslaughter, prompted Mr Justice Wilde to tell her she had killed her child by a constant course of ill-usage. 'You have been convicted of a very wicked and shameful act,' added the judge, 'and if I thought you had intended to kill the child, I would have made the punishment much more severe.' As it was, Mary Lincoln was ordered to serve three years' penal servitude. What happened to her during that time and after, is not known. Interestingly enough, the Christian names, age or occupation of little John Lincoln's father were not committed to the columns of the *Barnsley Chronicle*, despite the fact that he was called as a witness at the inquest hearing.

It seems either the courts or the Chronicle accepted that a social stigma was attached to infanticide and Mr Lincoln was referred to simply as 'the deceased's father'.

What is known about him is that he lost his first wife, the mother of his three children, some 14 weeks before John's death on April

30th. Approximately seven weeks later he married Mary.

She, it seems, could not have been too popular with her neighbours in Acklands — also spelled Acklam's — Row just off Joseph Street, in the Barebones area of Barnsley. Three of her neighbours seemed to have little reluctance in telling the inquest and the subsequent assize hearing of the violence she used against her newly-acquired charges.

Briefly summarised, their evidence to the inquest, held in New Street's Commercial Inn, was that she frequently beat all three children, sometimes using a metal buckled leather strap. John, aged four according to the inquest hearing and aged three according to the assize hearing, appeared to have suffered the worst. Having rickets, he was described as a 'child of dirty habits' which appears to have aggrieved his stepmother considerably.

The neighbours all reported that John appeared frightened to death of his stepmother – so much so that he accepted his beatings often without murmur.

Three days before John's death, the women said they were present when Mrs Lincoln complained about John being dirty, struck him with her fist at the back of his head and then threw him forcibly to the ground with the result that his head struck the stone

flagged floor hard. One of the three witnesses, a widow by the name of Catherine Peaker, told the trial that she had been summoned to look at one of John's thighs over two weeks earlier. The thigh was swollen and hard.

A few days later the other thigh became similarly swollen and the surgeon who conducted the post mortem examination later told the court that both thighs were broken, and had been so before the day of his death although, in his opinion, the fractures had occurred at different times.

Mrs Peaker told the court that, on the day of the child's death, she had heard Mrs Lincoln administering a beating to John. Very soon after the blows had stopped, and before anyone had had time to take the child upstairs, she saw Mrs Lincoln run with the boy to another neighbour's house, claiming that the eldest son had allowed him to fall down the stairs. The elder boy, she said, had been playing in the yard, while the beating was being administered. There is no record of the boy ever giving evidence to the court, although he did give evidence to the inquest when the coroner, Mr T. Taylor, made out a warrant for Mrs Lincoln's committal to York Assizes, following the jury's unanimous verdict that she was guilty of an act of manslaughter.

The boy's evidence to the inquest was such that a Chronicle reporter of the day commented, 'It was quite evident that he had been tutored what to say. He persisted that he had let the child fall down the stairs, but certain portions of his evidence were so contradictory that not the slightest reliance could be placed on it.'

Mrs Lincoln was not legally represented at her trial when the surgeon, Mr Blackburn, testified that the child had died of a haemorrhage following a fractured skull. Her evidence was simply that the child's legs were injured before her marriage and that she had consulted Mr Blackburn about it and had been told that his legs were not broken but that the child was 'rickety'.

The fact that she was not represented helped split the people of Barnsley down the middle in their views on the case. Some considered she was as unfortunate as the child, being an immature young woman suddenly faced with the prospect of caring for a husband and three young children, one of them in a poor state of health. Others considered Mary Lincoln an evil woman who, not only killed a disadvantaged and defenceless child, but then tried to worm her way out of it by blaming an eight year old.

The choice is yours.

Victim: ***Henry Chadwick, beaten,*** **May 1862**

Henry Chadwick's death at the hands of John Jackson was a mystery when it took place in May 1862 and, in some respects, remains so to this day. It is a mystery because no one, other than the two parties involved, saw it take place or knew why it took place and certainly Henry Chadwick was not left in a position to throw much light on the matter. Indeed, had it not been for a boast-like statement from Jackson, the crime could have become one of those classic mysteries delved into by several local historians over the years with no satisfactory conclusions drawn.

As it was, Jackson's boast resulted in his trial at York Assizes, although he was subsequently acquitted on the Judge's direction for lack of evidence.

The story starts in earnest at approximately 3 a.m. on Wednesday, May 21st, when four young men, returning from Barnsley Fair to Dodworth, found Chadwick lying insensible in the road. They half-carried and half-dragged him for a while before deciding he was drunk and again depositing him on the floor. But Chadwick, a 34-year-old weaver and corporal in the Barnsley Rifle Corps, was not drunk and did in fact tell them that he had been attacked by an unnamed assailant.

That was virtually all Chadwick was able to say about the incident. His brain was haemorrhaging, as the quartet might have realised had they seen the blood trickling from his ear. He died on the Friday morning. Oddly enough, his skull was not fractured.

An inquest was held the following day at the Gate Inn, Dodworth, when Chadwick's widow, Hannah, of Needful Cottage, Dodworth Road, told the court that Chadwick was not a quarrelsome man, nor was he accustomed to fighting. Her plight of fending for four young children was realised by the *Barnsley Chronicle*, which said in its report, 'Let us hope that he who tempereth the wind to the shorn lamb and gives the young ravens their food will vouch for the bereaved widow the means of providing for their wants, a task so delightful for the maternal heart'.

The evidence which connected Jackson, a Dodworth sexton and dayman at Pogmoor's Strafford Main Colliery, with the offence was given by Charles Saville, a Pogmoor engine worker, who told the hearing that he reproached Jackson for arriving late for work at 'nigh on 6 o'clock' on the morning of the attack. The latter replied, 'The less you say to me the better, or I'll do to thee same as I've done to yond other bugger... Knock thee down and punch thee up again'.

Mr Saville knew nothing of the attack on Mr Chadwick at that time. Jackson later told another witness that he had met Chadwick between the last house in Dodworth Road and the old bar house and that Chadwick had asked him to fight. Jackson claimed that he put up his fists and gave Chadwick 'something for himself' before he left.

The Coroner explained that, even if a man was obliged to fight in self-defence, he had no right to use more violence than was necessary for his own protection, and nothing could justify kicking a man when on the ground. The jury took just five minutes to return a verdict of manslaughter against John Jackson. The Coroner then made out a warrant for his committal for trial at York Assizes, but allowed Jackson bail.

He had to wait two months to learn his fate, but was spared the agony of a long trial. After hearing similar evidence to that at the inquest, the judge interposed and said that there did not seem to be any possibility of making out a case against the prisoner. It could not be shown who had struck the fatal blow and it could have been that the deceased had been drunk and quarrelsome, or possibly had suffered injury before fighting with the defendant.

Drunk and quarrelsome maybe, but Henry Chadwick, who had spent the last twelve months of his life as a coal screener despite being a linen weaver by trade, seems to have been popular. The Chronicle's report of his funeral states that 'some thousands in number' lined the route of the funeral procession from Barnsley to Dodworth. The march was led by 'brother musicians and members of the Rifle Corps', who proceeded in full military array with the band playing the Dead March from 'Saul'.

One piece of information that was never made clear at either hearing, was whether the two men knew each other before that chance meeting on the fateful night.

The judge's supposition that Mr Chadwick may have been drunk and quarrelsome was not supported by evidence given to the inquest by Dodworth weaver, Mr John Nixon, who said Chadwick was sober when he saw him outside Barnsley's Dusty Miller Inn in Pontefract Road between 1 and 2 a.m. on the morning of his death. He said that Chadwick was a quiet man, but would fight if anyone struck him.

Jackson's version of the incident, and the fact that he walked off leaving Chadwick unconscious or semi-conscious, and boasted of the matter only hours later, would hardly enhance his reputation as a man.

But he seemed to have had no motive for killing Chadwick, and the latter's lack of injuries other than cuts and bruises seemed to indicate a fight had taken place rather than a violent attack. As further confirmation, it seems Chadwick was found with his jacket and waistcoat off and with his braces tied round his waist, indicating that he was prepared in advance for a fight.

Was, then, Henry Chadwick the architect of his own death by pressing for a fight which he lost? Or did he, as the judge believed possible, meet someone else on his way home from the Dusty Miller that night? The only other explanation is that Jackson escaped a possible prison sentence by withholding the whole truth or perhaps even interchanging their roles.

Victim: ***Henry Baslow, beaten,*** **July 1877**

John Clarke had anything but violence on his mind when he went to bed on the night of Sunday, July 22th 1877. The 25-year-old gardener had retired upstairs with his wife at her mother's home in Shafton when the peace of the night was shattered by the arrival of Henry Baslow. Within minutes the two men were fighting and it was Baslow who came off the worst.

Why Baslow, a 52-year-old miner in a 'noisy and intoxicated state', chose to visit the home of widow, Sarah Ann Rowley, is not known. But it is known that the visit was not welcome and it was to be one of the last social calls he ever made. By Tuesday, July 31th, he was dead. He had died in his lodgings in Wincover, Royston, unattended by a doctor having said nothing about the reason for his visit and little about the fight itself.

Baslow's death resulted in the arrest of Clarke, described as 'tall and somewhat slender' and his conveyance by Inspector Crawshaw to the inquest hearing, held before coroner Mr F H Taylor at Royston's Ship Inn.

The first person to give evidence was 'coalgetter' James Crummack, who lodged with Baslow and said he knew him as a strong and healthy underground labourer, 'considering his age'. On the 21st, he had been to Shafton Feast with Baslow and Sam Laughton, before calling at the Fox and Hounds where they had two quarts of porter and ginger beer mixed. Baslow was talking to some sinkers when Crummack left for home at around 9pm.

The next time he saw Baslow was at 3pm the following day when he noticed his right eye was cut and swollen and asked him about it. Baslow's reply was simply that a gardener had done it. He wasn't sober at that time, but between then and his death, he was not drunk. Although unable to work, he was up and about and, on the day of his death, had been outside the house before he began breathing hard and complaining of pains in his head and chest. He then retired to bed with a mustard plaster on his chest.

Barnsley surgeon Mr J Blackburn, told the court Baslow's

external injuries included a black eye, bloodshot eyeball, an open wound above his right eyebrow and bruising to his chest and scrotum. He believed great force would have been required to produce such injuries.

Removal of the skullcap, however, revealed distended membranes and blood vessels congested with blood, while examination of the chest showed a fractured rib and evidence that one lung had been badly diseased for some years. The cause of death was inflammation of the membranes of the brain, with serious effusion caused by direct violence but accelerated by the fractured rib and disease of the lung.

Among those who witnessed the fight was Henry Thorpe who said he and Baslow had been drinking beer at the home of Charles Padley, after leaving the Fox and Hounds but Baslow had left them half an hour earlier. Baslow, Mrs Rowley and Clarke were involved in noisy debate with the latter complaining that Baslow had been beating on the door. The argument turned to violence when Clarke tried to return to the door and was thrown to the ground by Baslow.

Despite suffering a head wound, Clarke struck Baslow three or four times. The first blow, the witness claimed, resulted in Baslow falling against a wall. Subsequent blows were struck while he was on the ground. Clarke then entered the house and the door was locked. Thorpe left Baslow sitting on the causeway in the company of pit sinker, John Wiltshire.

Mrs Rowley, however, told a different story. She said the only blow she saw was Baslow's blow to Firth, but she admitted falling over the men as they were struggling on the ground, dropping her young grandson as a result.

The Ship Inn, Royston where the inquest on Henry Baslow was held.

Mrs Rowley admitted knowing Baslow but nothing more. She said she had heard a 'drunken man', approaching the house and immediately fastened the door. However, Baslow then looked through the window.

'I asked him what he wanted and why he wanted to annoy me,' she said. 'He then shook the window so much that I thought it would come out. I told him to go away but he said that he would go when he was ready.'

It was then that Clarke arrived downstairs, put his trousers on and opened the door to Baslow saying:

'Well Harry – what ar thar doing here?'

After the fight, she begged Baslow to go away and got Clarke back into the house.

Shafton miner Charles Padley said Baslow left his home at 11.40pm on the night of the fight and that he did not see him until 11o'clock the following morning, when he turned up with a cut eye and cheek. He knew both men and said Baslow had told him that he had 'caught it more than he had ever done before', while Clarke described it as a 'falling out', with Baslow.

Baslow's only real account of the incident came from Andrew Bamforth, a Shafton miner, who said Baslow appeared at his home three hours after the fight, 'as if he had come out of a slaughterhouse.'

Sitting in a chair and refusing an offer to wash his wounds, Baslow told him a gardener had caused his injuries saying he had 'done him', although he had been 'as hard as stone.' He also said, 'He kicked me like a ball'.

Bearing in mind that none of the witnesses had mentioned the involvement of another man, Baslow had apparently then made a surprising claim that a man had been with him at the time, but he had run away adding, 'more's the pity.' He likened the departure of the mystery man as, 'that a greyhound could not catch him'.

Baslow, claimed Padley, believed the fight took place at around 12.30am and explained the time lapse by saying he was so sore that he could not stir.

In his summing-up, the coroner told the jury that householders had the right to remove people making a nuisance of themselves from their homes but, had more force been used than necessary, could face prosecution themselves... up to and including manslaughter.

'If you feel the deceased's injuries were such as would not of themselves have been fatal but have been rendered fatal by the man's own imprudence and unjustifiable mode of living then, undoubtedly, no one would be responsible of it,' he said.

'But so far as he understood the doctor and so far as the law was concerned, if the man was suffering from any complaint and that complaint was aggravated so as to cause death by injuries received, then that was manslaughter.' It was not, he added, part of the the jury's role to inquire on the degree of punishment to be inflicted on the person who had caused the death of the deceased.

Jurors James Littlewood, John Walter Rhodes, John Peckett, George Wilson, John Bayldon, John Sandbury, Abra Watson, James Simpson, John Oldroyd, Jonathan Dransfield, John Hill and Charles Cutts retired for 40 minutes before returning with a verdict of manslaughter against John Clarke. That decision meant John Clarke had to wait a full eight months before his case was heard at a West Riding Division Crown Court hearing, before Mr Justice Hawkins at Leeds Town Hall. He then pleaded guilty after a brief outline of the facts by a Mr Barker, prosecuting. Perhaps because of time spent on remand, Clarke found the judge sympathetic and was discharged.

The Barnsley public were left to puzzle about the identity of the alleged third man and the reason for their late-night visit to Mrs Rowley's home. Those living outside Shafton could also puzzle as to the scene of the altercation which led to the bloody encounter because, bizarrely, no mention was made of Mrs Rowley's address in the *Barnsley Chronicle*.

Also interesting, is the fact that Mrs Rowley was not asked how she knew the deceased or, indeed, how her son-in-law knew him. Clarke, it seems, knew Baslow well enough to address him by his Christian name, but curiously, Baslow's knowledge of him seemed limited to the fact that he was a gardener.

On reflection, it is easy to sympathise with the defendant. He was, we know, simply trying to get a good night's sleep, when the peace was shattered by a man whose comments later seem to indicate he had always been perfectly capable of looking after himself during similar encounters in the past. But while Baslow seems to have struck the first blow, it does seem that with five separate head wounds, not to mention his black eye, broken ribs and bruised scrotum, he suffered a pretty forceful beating for a man of his age.

Perhaps the old saying about sleeping dogs should also apply to sleeping gardeners.

Victim: ***George Broadhead,* 1878**

George Broadhead lost his life as a result of horseplay which turned nasty. The 22-year-old miner was walking to his Monk Bretton home late on the night of January 19th 1878, when his hat was snatched from his head by 17-year-old miner, Walter Hadfield, Bennett who like him, had spent the evening drinking with friends.

Broadhead's reaction was to seize the hat of one of Bennett's friends and refuse to return it until his own was returned.

Such stand-off situations between two groups of men usually end peacefully but this one didn't. The reason was that Bennett ran off with Broadhead's hat while his friend, William Marsh, demanded the return of his cap. Marsh, a 20-year-old collier punched Broadhead to the ground and kicked him, before Bennett returned to the scene and joined in the attack.

The violence was eventually stopped through the intervention of others and shouts that a policeman was approaching but by then, the damage was done. Broadhead had to be carried home by friends to his young wife. He was never well enough to work again and it soon became apparent he would never fully recover from the attack. Appreciation of that however, meant he had another meeting with his attackers before his death on February 27th.

Marsh and Bennett were taken to Broadhead's home by Superintendent Sykes to hear him make a deposition to Mr W Carrington, Clerk to Barnsley Magistrates. The deposition read:

'I am a miner by trade and reside at Smithy Wood, Monk Bretton.

'I am very ill and have no hopes of recovery. I have Dr Lancaster attending me. I really think I am going to die.'

'Three weeks ago last night, I was in Barnsley. Robert Challenger and John Medley were with me. We got in Sheffield Road and the man Bennett, now here, took my hat off. I took another hat off one of Bennett's mate's head.

'I went up to Bennett for my hat and then somebody punched me - I mean kicked me.

'They got me down on the ground, they kicked me down. I don't know whether either William Marsh or Walter Bennett, the two men here present, kicked me or not. I could not recollect the others that were there.'

Bennett and Marsh, who had been arrested and charged with unlawful wounding the day after the attack, also attended the inquest hearing held at the Royal Arms, Smithies on March 1st. The jury there decided Broadhead died of injuries received from kicking, but said there was insufficient evidence to identify the person by whom the injuries were inflicted.

A charge of manslaughter was preferred at a committal hearing held, unusually, in Barnsley's Town Hall two days later before Mr F H Taylor and Mr J Dyson.

That hearing heard Barnsley surgeon W J Lancaster, state death was due to inflammation of the brain caused by a fractured skull and that the injury was 'likely' caused by kicking from a boot. Detective Sergeant Brown told how he arrested the men the day after the incident. Marsh was immediately contrite saying:

'I am sorry – I was fighting with him about a quarter of an hour and, if he had not got it, I should.'

But Bennett protested his innocence saying:

'I only went between Marsh and Broadhead to separate them.'

That claim, however, suffered great damage from the evidence of two independent witnesses, Henry Barraclough of Roper Street and Thomas Shepherd, of Pitt Street. Both testified to Bennett emerging from an alley linking Sheffield Road with Pontefract Road, shouting' 'Where is he?' before kicking the man Marsh had been fighting.

Bennett and Marsh were both represented by Mr Freeman, who contended that there was insufficient evident with which to commit the prisoners on a charge of manslaughter, but that was rejected by the magistrates who committed them for trial at the Yorkshire Assizes with bail surety set at £40 each. Their appearance before Mr Justice Hawkins at Leeds on April 8th, saw Mr Barker, prosecuting, tell how Broadhead and his friends overtook the prisoners in Sheffield Road at around 11.30pm and how the fight developed near the Corporation Hotel.

He said the taking of caps started as a joke, but soured as a result of Marsh becoming angry and asking for the return of his hat several times. Bennett's arrival from the alley, presumably that later known as Primrose Hill, was accompanied by words of encouragement to Marsh, 'Go into him. We can lace the whole lot of them'.

The hapless victim was then 'savagely' kicked by both men while on the ground. Mr Barker added that Broadhead remained in bed until the Friday of the following week. On the Saturday, he went to work but was unable to stop and again took to his bed.

The *Barnsley Chronicle* said of the hearing:

'Substantially there was no defence. The jury found them guilty but strongly recommended them to mercy.'

Sentencing was deferred to the Wednesday when the judge remarked that in some districts of the West Riding 'outrages' of a similar kind were very common and men had too little regard for the persons and limbs of others and thought they could commit acts like this with impunity. But that would not be the case, he added, while he was sitting. Bennett and Marsh were sentenced to twelve months imprisonment with hard labour.

No doubt George Broadhead would have jumped at the chance of exchanging his fate for their's.

The Corporation Hotel in the 1960s. Some eighty years earlier a bout of horseplay turned nasty and in the ensuing fight, which took place in Pontefract Road, a young miner received injuries from which he later died.

Victim: ***Baby Parkin, battered,*** **August 1884**

It was on August 11th, 1884, that 12-year-old William Henry Kaye was preparing to bathe in a local stream when he made the most gruesome discovery of his life. Aided by his friends John Broadhead and John William Smeaton, he waded in water up to his neck to pull a wet bundle to the bank. They then discovered that the doll-like bundle was, in fact, the decomposing body of a baby girl.

Showing great maturity for his years, Kaye later delivered the child, which was dressed in a long white nightgown and bib, into the arms of P.C. George Dales. The body was taken from the brook at Crow Nest, Stainborough, to the Strafford Arms Hotel, where an inquest was held the following day.

A verdict of 'Found Dead' was returned by the jury and the unidentified body delivered into the custody of Herbert Parker for interment at Barnsley Cemetery. Ten days later the body of the hapless mite was exhumed by order of the Home Secretary, following the arrest of a 26-year-old Dodworth woman, Ann Parkin.

Parkin, a single woman, was duly charged with the wilful murder of her six-week-old, but unnamed, daughter. The main evidence against her came from Martha Jane Hawksworth, a 38-year-old widow, of Grace Street, Barnsley, who had informed the police that Parkin arrived at her home early on the evening of July 2nd saying that her parents were dead and that she had no place to go.

At 11 p.m. that same night, Parkin gave birth to a baby girl at her new lodgings. From then until August 5th, Mrs Hawksworth and her friend, Ann Kenworthy, nursed both mother and child and even loaned baby clothes.

At 6 p.m. on August 5th, Parkin left the house and at 9.45 p.m. arrived at the home of her brother, James, in Dodworth Bottom, without the child but with a shawl loaned by Mrs Hawksworth. It was the possession of that shawl, duly identified by Mrs Hawksworth, as were the nightgown and bib subsequently, that was

to form a damning indictment against Parkin and lead to sentence of death being passed on her.

The other evidence that was to ensure that Parkin paid dearly for infanticide was the fact that the baby had not been drowned. Surgeon Mr J. Blackburn determined by post mortem examination that there were eight fractures to the skull of the illegitimate child and that death took place before immersion. Parkin pleaded not guilty to wilful murder when she appeared before Mr Baron Pollock at York Assizes on November 17th.

She had always maintained her innocence. When arrested by Detective Sergeant William Lodge and charged with the offence, she said: 'I didn't kill it. I was going over the fields to Stainborough, I missed my way and fell into the water with my child and I lost it'.

Her counsel, also named Blackburn, managed to elicit from the surgeon, Mr Blackburn, that the head injuries could have been caused by her falling on the child and rolling over. But the fact that she still had the shawl in her possession, had not recovered the body or reported the death seemingly did little to impress the jury.

They took just 35 minutes before returning to the court with a verdict of 'guilty'. Having heard evidence that Parkin's parents had refused to accept her at home because of the misfortune that had befallen her, they did however couple their verdict with a strong recommendation for mercy.

They watched Parkin, described as 'pale and trembling', as the judge placed the black cap on his head and said: 'I don't think that any words of mine could be of any use, either with regard to the public, or those who have heard the trial of this case or yourself, except to remind you that I do hope that in the ensuing time that will remain to you, you will use that time looking for pardon and peace where pardon and peace alone can be found.

Despite that sentence of death, which resulted in the defendant almost being carried from the dock in a fainting condition, the jury's plea for mercy was eventually honoured. The death sentence was later commuted to one of penal servitude and according to a Lodge's Almanack of 1907, Ann Parkin was released from prison in January 1897, after serving a twelve year sentence.

To some, Ann Parkin must rate as a heartless woman who bludgeoned her child to death without mercy. To others, she will rank as an unfortunate victim of a Victorian era which had little sympathy for those whose lives were a greyer shade of white. In support of the latter, both Mrs Hawksworth and her friend Mrs Kenworthy gave evidence that Parkin was depressed and despondent after the birth and was secretive about herself.

Those taking the harder line, however, will point out the fact that several days elapsed between the disappearance of the child and young master Kay's bathing expedition. For most of that time the brook, winding its way from Silkstone Common to feed Worsbrough reservoir, was little more than a trickle. But on Saturday, August 9th, 1884, the Barnsley area was subjected to a two-hour thunderstorm, which resulted in a 'ball of fire' striking one house in Somerset Street. As a result of the deluge, the stream was transformed into a raging torrent, and it is just possible that the 'fresh' resulted in a little baby's body being flushed out from a concealed hiding place.

They would perhaps argue that God acted in an appropriate way to disclose the fate of an unnamed and unloved little innocent.

Victim: ***Richard Dugdale knifed and beaten,*** **October 1884**

Richard Dugdale's murder was later described by a judge as 'most cruel'... It was. Not only had the respected Barnsley man been beaten so badly that one eye was out of its socket, but his throat had been cut so forcefully that his larynx and vertebrae had been severed. It was not surprising therefore that the words: 'Done through anxiety of mind – Good bye', found written on the flyleaf of a notebook belonging to Dugdale, failed in its purpose to indicate suicide. The man who a jury decided did write it could have been described as writing his own epitaph. He was a 25-year-old borer of Bolton, Lancashire, by the name of Kay Howarth. He was also a man who repaid kindness and generosity with treachery.

The fact that Richard Lee Dugdale had lived the last 18 months of his 37 years in Wakefield, and that the murder took place in Bolton, did little to diminish Barnsley's interest in the gruesome event. The *Barnsley Chronicle* devoted almost half a page of its October 11, 1884 edition to the crime. Mr Dugdale was well known to them and to the rest of the town, having worked in the railway goods office, for the founders of Barnsley Brewery, Paul and Guy Senior and for a Hoyle Mill maltster by the name of Locke, before accepting a position as traveller to Castleford-based maltsters, Messrs Austin Brothers. He was also a stalwart of the Friendly Societies, a sort of election agent for James Lund and a member of the recently formed Hospital Sunday movement. But it was probably in his work for the Barnsley Branch of the Ancient Order of Foresters, who met in the Queens Hotel, that he was best remembered. While he held the position of Worthy Chief Ranger, a procession of Barnsley dignitaries, including Barnsley's M.P. of 1884, W.S. Stanthope, had applied for membership. Others included Alderman Newman, Alderman Carter and Richard Innes.

Dugdale had travelled to Bolton on a business trip on Wednesday October 1st. His body was found on waste land behind a warehouse at 9 p.m. on Friday October 3rd. Five o'clock the following morning saw the arrest of Howarth – his clothes besmeared with blood, knuckles swollen and pocket full of money. On the Monday Howarth was described as showing a 'cool and stolid demeanor' as he heard evidence of the events on the Friday given to the inquest.

The most damning evidence was given by an oil merchant named Robert Hall, who said he had spent most of the day drinking with Mr Dugdale and Howarth in various public houses. After being refused service in one public house because of their drunken condition, Dugdale complained of feeling sick and set off for his hotel in the company of Howarth. A short time later, Howarth returned on his own. Not having had time to walk Dugdale all the way there, he merely claimed Dugdale had changed his mind about needing accompanying. Howarth, claimed Mr Hall, had been without money throughout the afternoon and Dugdale had purchased all his drinks for him.

But one Charles Leonard, who lodged with Howarth, said he met up with him at 9 p.m. that night in Bolton Theatre, and Howarth was in the best box, his pockets full of gold. After the theatre, Howarth treated Leonard and another man to at least three brandies and a fish and potato supper. He explained his swollen knuckles and possession of cash saying he had had to punch a man in the face after a game of dominoes to collect his winnings. He also claimed that he didn't owe a living man a 'cent'. As Dugdale died around 7 p.m., that statement, at least, appears to have been true.

Howarth maintained his unemotional manner when he appeared before magistrates later the same day. This time he heard three teenage girls who said that they had seen him with Dugdale near the scene of the murder shortly before 7 p.m.

Howarth claimed Dugdale had entrusted the £32.10s in gold, 18s in silver, a cheque for £8 and a gold watch and chain to him for safe keeping, because of the possibility that he could fall down and be

robbed. He denied evidence from witnesses that the knife found in the victim's hand was his own and tried to explain his bruised knuckles by his cross examination of Elijah Hargreaves, landlord of the Fleece Hotel.

'Did you see me strike a man in the mouth after a game of dominoes?' he asked. 'Yes', replied Mr Hargreaves, 'and I thought it very cowardly of you. You waited for Mr Dugdale to come in and called him 'a friend' before striking the man'. Mr Hargreaves, however, denied that he had seen Howarth gain any money as a result of the assault.

The trial of Kay Howarth on the charge of the wilful murder of Richard Dugdale lasted from 10 a.m. to 9 p.m. at Manchester Assizes on November 4 – a marathon by the standards of those days. At its end, the jury took just 20 minutes to find Howarth guilty. Howarth, who was unrepresented, remained 'passive and cool', even when Mr Justice Smith told the jury their verdict was the only one they could have returned on the evidence and sentenced him to death.

When asked if he had anything to say, however, he maintained he was innocent. Howarth, without a witness on his behalf, maintained throughout that Dugdale had given him his possessions for safe keeping. But he was unable to explain the blood on Mr Dugdale's watch, the blood on his clothes or the knife. It was also highly unlikely that footpads would have written those words in Dugdale's pocketbook, although Howarth never made any reference to them. The words were, incidentally, far different from the businessman-like entries in the rest of the book.

There seems, therefore, little doubt that Howarth, who claimed to have been to America and returned, was guilty of a bloody and unprovoked murder despite his denials. But it also seems that Dugdale contributed to his own departure from this life by an astonishingly bad judgement of character, for a man so highly regarded in Barnsley circles.

Asked by a juror at the inquest why a man like Howarth was with him and Mr Dugdale, Robert Hall said he had not wanted Howarth with them, and considered him to be what would today be termed a 'free-loader', preying on the generosity of visiting commercial travellers.

But Mr Hall added that, when he expressed that view to Mr Dugdale, the latter replied: 'He seems a decent man'! Hours later he was dead by those same hands which had so eagerly accepted his free drinks.

Victim: ***Police Constable Alfred Austwick, shot* July 1886**

Detective Sergeant William Lodge's arrest of murderer William Murphy must rank as one of the bravest arrests ever – or most foolhardy. The moustachioed police officer made his way up the steps of a house in Kingstone Place knowing his man had already killed one police officer and escaped an attempted arrest by levelling a shotgun at another. He also knew, as he kicked open the bedroom door, that the mind of Murphy, who had spent six weeks playing a deadly game of hide and seek with the police, was unhinged.

The detective sergeant found himself looking down the barrel of Murphy's gun but he didn't flinch. Instead he produced his umbrella and prodded the gun which discharged its deadly contents into the ceiling. As the plaster showered them both, other police officers rushed in to restrain Murphy and thereby ended one of the biggest manhunts Barnsley had ever seen.

Public interest in the murder of P.C. Austwick at Dodworth on the fateful night of July 31st, 1886 was so great that the *Barnsley Chronicle* produced a 'Special Gratis' supplement shortly before the subsequent trial at York in November of that year. The skills of artists and engravers were called on to illustrate Murphy, his capture, the house where he made his earlier escape from arrest, his captor, his prosecutor and, of course, his hapless victim.

One factor which fuelled the interest in the case was that Murphy, an ex-poacher, had led the police a merry chase by living rough and making a daring escape by leaping out of a window when cornered at his brother-in-law's home in Barugh Green. Another was the allegation that the murder victim had waged a virtual vendetta against Murphy for several years. P.C. Austwick, a large, bearded ex-railway signalman probably had good reason to suspect Murphy of every felony which took place in Dodworth. The latter had first offended back in 1862 and by 1886 had amassed a total of 26 offences, including a housebreaking one at Batley which was punished by five years of back-breaking penal servitude. But it was probably Austwick's method of getting at Murphy which most enraged him. The officer would often stop Murphy's children in the street, quiz them and then store away the knowledge for future use.

On the afternoon of July 31st, Murphy had been drinking at Dodworth's Station Hotel where he showed the landlord a summons that P.C. Austwick had served on him. 'He has served this on me but he will never have to serve another because I will blow a hole through him,' said Murphy.

At 11 p.m. that night, Murphy and several other men left the Fountain Inn. Twenty minutes later P.C. Austwick arrived and studied the men's faces in the beam of his torch. At that, Murphy's mind snapped. 'You are the man I want – stop there!' he shouted. Then he dashed to his mother's home in nearby Lambert Fold to collect his gun. A few minutes later a shot was heard and P.C. Austwick collapsed in the gutter outside Buckle's butcher's shop in Green Road with a massive three-inch wound in the chest. Two hours later he was dead.

Murphy fled immediately and successfully evaded the huge police dragnet for the next five weeks, living for some of the time at least

Interior of the Crown Court at York.

in the centre of a cornfield. He was eventually tracked to his brother-in-law's seedy tenement in Barugh Green where he made his successful escape attempt by leaping through a window. It took another week for the police to accomplish the arrest with the help of D.S. Lodge and his umbrella.

When the trial started at York Assizes the court was packed with people, 'all eager to look at the notorious man,' according to newspaper reports. Murphy's notoriety had spread throughout the county and probably the country. The defence case hinged on the state of Murphy's mind and the vendetta conducted by the policeman, but that appeared to find little favour with the judge who said, 'If insanity were proved by crime, few people would be held responsible for the acts they committed'.

Perhaps, not surprisingly, the jury returned a verdict of guilty without leaving the court and James Murphy was hanged at York in November 1886.

By today's standards, that plea of insanity could well have succeeded. There was evidence to show that Murphy was unhinged, including the words he shouted as he fired the fatal shot, 'Where are we now?' And it may be that at least one juror sympathised with his case. Half-way through the judge's summing up, a York chemist named Thompson, rose from his juror's seat. His Lordship ordered him to sit back down and he complied, but a short while later, Thompson made some comment to the judge. He was ordered to hold his tongue or he would be committed to prison for contempt of court. Mr Thompson persisted and he was fined the considerable sum for those days of £6. Unfortunately, exactly what Mr Thompson said, or tried to say, was not reported – and we shall never know.

That, you would think, would be the end of the story of James Murphy but perhaps the most interesting insight into the man was contained in the *Barnsley Chronicle* columns of April 23rd, 1892, when the noted executioner, James Berry, published a book about his work. He described Murphy as a man without fear, who had a hearty appetite and cheerful disposition to the end – so much so that he even expressed great interest in the pinion mechanism of the gallows. But while Murphy regarded his sentence and execution 'rather as a joke and a matter of pride', the Roman Catholic priests attending him could get no satisfaction out of him whatsoever.

Murphy, incidentally, did not get his last request – a pipeful of 'bacca'.

What follows is reproduced from the *Barnsley Chronicle* Supplement of Saturday October 2nd, 1886.

POLICE-CONSTABLE ALFRED AUSTWICK, the unfortunate victim of Murphy's malignant hate, was born at Lumby, a pretty little rural hamlet near Selby, in the parochial district of South Milford. His parents before him resided at Lumby, where his father has been employed since 1854, about the time of the birth of his murdered son Alfred, in the service of Mr Webster and his son, as farm bailiff. He had but one brother, who was crushed to death against a wall by a horse, about five years ago. There is one sister, who still survives, and who was in Barnsley on the day of the hearing, along with her aged father and Mrs Austwick. Alfred in his early days attended the Wesleyan School at South Milford, afterwards being for some time a scholar at Thorpe Arch School. As he came nearer to man's estate, he was for a time in the employ of a railway company at South Milford, and when about 19 years of age he joined the West-Riding Constabulary. After spending the usual time at the Depot, Wakefield, he came to Barnsley in the latter part of 1873. After serving about twelve months in Barnsley he was removed to Gawber, where he was stationed till 1875, when he experienced another move and was placed at Worsbro' Dale. Being now between twenty-two and twenty-three years old, he became dissatisfied about something or other and left the force, and returned to Lumby.

Mr Brown, who is now station-master at the South Milford Junction on the North-Eastern Railway, and who has known the deceased and his parents all his life, was at that time inspector of the Selby district of the railway, and the deceased applied to him for a situation as a signalman. Mr Brown reasoned with deceased, suggesting to him that he was making a mistake in leaving the service in which he had been for some years. He, however, said he was tired of police duties, and thought he should be more settled if he had a situation on the railway in his own district. The result was he was engaged, and deceased, like the rest of the employees, was called to pass under the standard. No one taller than six feet had been arranged for, however, and considerable amusement was caused by the efforts of some shorter men to mark the chalk the height of the stalwart young servant. As a signalman, Austwick was sent to Goole, where he spent some time in the service of the company. While here he formed the acquaintance of Miss Sarah Goulton, his future wife, and was married to her in 1876 or 1877. For some time after his marriage he remained in the service of the Railway Company, but eventually sent in his resignation, and, on the 24th October, 1881, he again joined the West-Riding Constabulary. A few weeks later, on the 1st December, 1881, he was sent to Dodworth in succession to P.C. Longley, who had resigned on superannuation allowance, and there he was stationed until his murder. Whilst living at Dodworth Austwick gained universal esteem by his general conduct and good nature. His family increased to seven children, but two of them died suddenly some time ago, and were interred in Dodworth Churchyard.

JAMES MURPHY, who now lies in Wakefield Gaol on the charge of wilfully murdering Police-constable Alfred Austwick under circumstances with which our readers are all familiar, is, as we have said, a native of Barnsley. His age has hitherto been given as 43, but we have just ascertained that he is some three years older. He was born in what is now known as Court No. 9, New-street, on October 3rd, 1840, and consequently he will to-morrow complete his 46th year. He was baptized the day after his birth, by the Rev. John Rigby, the then rector of

Holyrood Catholic Church. Of his early years comparatively little is known. He was the son of a linen hand-loom weaver, and when some eight or ten years old his parents removed with their family to Dodworth. The father died there, about ten years ago, at the ripe age of 86 years, in a small tenement on the north side of High-street, a short distance from what used to be known as the Old Hall. His mother, whose maiden name was Flood, died last year in Barnsley Workhouse. There were five children, four boys and one girl. James was brought up to work in the pit, and ultimately became a coal getter, and as such he had the reputation of being a good workman. He, however, at an early age, took to evil ways, and in the course of time become a noted poacher. His first conviction was on the 14th June, 1862, when he was fined 10s. and costs, by Messrs Thomas Taylor and H. Jackson, at Barnsley Court House, for a game trespass on the land of Mr Thomas Edward Taylor, at Dodworth. His last conviction for poaching was on the 6th May, 1885, when he was charged, along with Matthew Foulstone, with a game trespass at Cawthorne, and fined 20s, his companion being fined 10s, and costs. He has also been charged with drunkenness and other offences, his convictions at Barnsley alone numbering twenty-five, while the times he has been before the magistrates are in all about thirty-six. He was also convicted, in 1878, at Batley, of housebreaking, and sentenced to five years' penal servitude. He has a wife and two children, a son and a daughter. Of how he spent his time during the six weeks odd that he was in hiding from the police we have only a fragmentary knowledge. The woman Bailey has given a list of several visits which he paid to the house of his brother-in-law, Goss, at Barugh Green, and he has himself admitted that he had been in hiding in cornfields while the police were searching for him in the immediate vicinity. One of his lairs, or hiding places – at least it is supposed to be one – was discovered the other week in a cornfield belonging to Mr John W. Ownsworth, farmer, of Moor End. It was not at the edge, where the police would be likely to search, but right into the field, and near by were found some pieces of paper with crumbs of bread. He was taken to Wakefield from Barnsley on the night of the hearing before the magistrates, and will not be removed to York Castle until the opening of the Assizes next month.

GOSS'S HOUSE, BARUGH GREEN. The house occupied by Goss at Barugh Green, from which Murphy succeeded in making his escape on Wednesday, Sept. 15th, is an old and rather dilapidated-looking tenement. It stands on the right-hand side of the lane leading from Barugh Green proper to Barugh Bridge, and is the lowermost in a block of three cottages of a similar character, which stand some distance back from the road, with gardens in front. On the lower, or east side, stands the Wesleyan Chapel, a portion of which is seen in the picture. The chapel is separated from the cottage garden by a wall, and it has no back entrance. The rear of the cottage is shown in the view, and the upper window is the one

from which Murphy dropped, he alighting among the cabbages immediately below. The window is from 2 feet to 2 feet 6 inches wide by from 18 to 20 inches high, one half opening with a slide to the width of about 13 inches. The window ledge, which is a broad one, is from a foot to 18 inches above the chamber floor, and the top of the window is formed by the joist on which the rooftree rests. Outside, the bottom of the window is seven or eight feet from the ground. The wall over which Murphy leaped, after presenting his gun at Detective-sergeant Ramsden, is directly opposite the window, and is some four feet high. On the other side of the wall is a field in the occupation of Mr Smith, farmer, and once here Murphy was clear of all serious obstructions.

THE HOUSE OF THE CAPTURE. The house occupied by John Henderson, at Kinstone place, in which Murphy was captured on the morning of Friday, Sept. 17th, is the centre one of a block of three brick tenements, owned by Mr William Dyson, joiner and builder, and known as Dyson's Cottages. The block is on the left, or south, side of the road leading through Kingstone to Keresforth-hill, and stands back some distance from the road. At the rear is an enclosure occupied by Mr Dyson for purposes connected with his business, and the cottages are distinctly visible from the main road. The back door of Henderson's cottage opens into the kitchen, and immediately behind it is a door leading to the staircase. This door opens outwards, so that when the kitchen door is open the staircase door cannot be opened, but if the staircase door is

opened first then the kitchen door can be opened as well. There was about a dozen wooden steps leading to the chambers above. That in which Murphy was found, and which is depicted on the plan, is entered from the left on reaching the top of the stairs, and has two windows which overlook Mr Dyson's premises right on to Kingstone-road. The room is some nine feet square, and was on the day of the capture entirely destitute of furniture, with the exception of a small French bedstead in one corner, and a chair, as shown in the illustration. Murphy's clothes were laid on the floor, near the end of the bed.

DETECTIVE-SERGEANT WILLIAM LODGE, whose fortune it was to take the leading part in Murphy's capture, and who did so at the risk of his life, has been over twenty-one years in the force, having joined on the 9th January, 1865. After spending six weeks in the Depot at Wakefield, he was sent to Pateley Bridge, where he remained two years. On March 1, 1867, he was on his own application removed to Cudworth in Staincross Division, and stayed there over four years. In May, 1871, he was, on the request of Mr F.H. Taylor, J.P., moved to Darfield. In compliance with the wish of this gentleman, he was raised to the rank of acting sergeant on the 16th July, 1872, and was sent to Dungworth, in Sheffield Division. He was made full sergeant in November of the same year. In March, 1873, he notified his desire for a change, and was sent to Acomb, in Tadcaster Division, whence he went to Lindley, near Otley, remaining there on Leeds waterworks until the 1st August, 1876. He was afterwards successively at Staincliffe, near Dewsbury; Batley, Bingley, and Lightcliffe, near Halifax. In Sept., 1878, he was transferred to Barnsley as Detective-sergeant, and remained here in that capacity until April, 1883. From Barnsley he went to Crosshills, Skipton Division, and on May last he was transferred to Halifax, where he is now stationed. He came to this Division on special duty after the murder, and remained until Saturday last. He has rendered some good service in his time. He was in this Division in 1870, when the Thorncliffe riots took place, and was one of those who took part in the celebrated Tankersley

Park 'charge'. He was specially complimented by the Sheffield West-Riding Magistrates in November, 1872, upon the judgment which he displayed in connection with some riots at Bradfield, and the late Mr Supt. Sykes, of Barnsley, also complimented him by letter, advising him always to be cool and collected in times of the greatest excitement.

MR JOHN CARRINGTON, the solicitor instructed by the Treasury to prosecute in Murphy's case, is the only son of Mr William Carrington, clerk to the West-Riding Bench of Magistrates, Staincross Division. He received his early education at Holyrood Catholic School, and at the Grammar School, Barnsley, in which latter he was one of the Locke Scholars. Subsequently he studied at Mount St Mary's College, Derbyshire, from which he proceeded to Stonyhurst College, Lancashire. He was articled to Messrs Tyas & Co., solicitors, of this town, and, having passed the requisite examinations, was admitted a solicitor in February, 1883. Soon afterwards he commenced practice on his own account, and has already had a considerable amount of professional experience.

Victim: ***Mary Hazlehurst, battered,*** **March 1887**

Mary Ann Hazlehurst could never have been described as a faithful wife and certainly not in the Victorian Times of 1887. But, as far as is known, she only experienced group sex once, the result being that she died a horrific and sickening death, thrown down the stairs of her home and savagely and repeatedly kicked by her husband. It was a death that the people of Wombwell took a long time to live down. Many of them were accused of being worse than 'barbarians', by the High Court Judge who tried Isaac Hazlehurst.

The reasons for that were twofold.

First, Mary Hazlehurst, a 35-year-old woman who had a drink problem but was still described as 'clean and tidy as any woman who wore shoe leather', appears to have been taken advantage of to satisfy the lust of a group of Wombwell men.

The accounts of that fateful day of March 20, 1887, all state that she objected to her husband and his drinking companions arriving at their home, situated opposite the Junction Inn, to continue their Sunday lunchtime drinking session. Her objections were overruled and she finished up drunk, and the men satiated their passions with her while keeping her husband so occupied he didn't realise what was happening.

The second reason, and perhaps the most damning indictment on the population of Wombwell, is that several people knew a murderous attack was being inflicted on her just a short time later, but did nothing to help.

George Finney, a Wombwell collier, told a committal hearing that he passed the Hazlehurst home at 62 Junction Row around 7 p.m. on March 20th, when Isaac Hazlehurst was standing at the open door. His wife could be seen lying on the floor inside, moaning with pain. As Mr Finney passed he heard the following exchange of words started by Mrs Hazlehurst: 'I have done nothing wrong.'

'Thas hast done nothing right thee!'

'Oh, murder'! she groaned.

Turning to go back inside, Hazlehurst said: 'I will give thee murder though, yer **** thing!'

Mr Finney said he heard 'thumps' which he took to be kicks, then walked away, after noting three women standing listening at an adjacent house. When Samuel Unwin Round, a Wombwell tailor, passed the scene at 7.15 p.m., he said there were five or six men and a woman near the closed door of the Hazlehurst home. He heard Isaac Hazlehurst twice put the following question to his wife: 'Didn't I catch Leather in bed with you this afternoon, myself?' On both occasions the question was followed by kicks or blows and cries of pain. Mr Round told the same hearing he looked under the bottom of the door and saw the shadow of a foot kicking a body on the floor.

When he again passed the house at 9.10 p.m., he heard 'groans' from within. He mentioned these facts to Joseph Skidmore, the licensee of the Junction Inn, who was subsequently fined for supplying beer to the Hazlehurst home in breach of Sunday observance laws. His reply was: 'It's nowt uncommon', accompanied by a shrug of his shoulders.

Those facts led Mr Justice Grantham, officiating at the Yorkshire Spring Assizes in Leeds, to describe Messrs Finney and Round and others as 'arrant cowards', while lambasting the Wombwell populace in general. He found it 'almost incredible' that people should have looked on and listened while Mrs Hazlehurst died at the hands of the 'miserable prisoner', and said the door should have been broken down, even if barred, by anyone worthy of the name 'man or woman'. He went on: 'I do not believe that in any other country inhabitated by what they call barbarians, men could be found to act as they had acted to that poor woman.' The judge also called for the return of the pillory for the men who, he said, 'satiated their disgusting passions on Mrs Hazlehurst', and told Isaac Hazlehurst that, had he vented his anger on Samuel Leather, whom he described as 'arch fiend among fiends', then the latter would have gone to his doom without anyone regretting the loss of a man who was unworthy to live. Had he done that, he would also have made his prosecution extremely unlikely, as well as vindicating his wife's honour.

Harsh words for all concerned, you may think, but had the judge known all the facts, he might have been even harder in his condemnation.

It is very unlikely that he knew that Mary Ann Hazlehurst was shunned by the people of Wombwell even in death. For while a great crowd gathered to watch the unfortunate woman's funeral procession, only the closest of relatives actually followed the hearse.

It also appears that the coffin might never have been lowered into the sanctuary of Wombwell Cemetery had not Mr Robinson, clerk to the Board of Health, instructed some of the board's labourers to assist in carrying it to the grave.

Meanwhile, the town's clergy seemed unanimous in expressing pity and sympathy for Isaac Hazlehurst while condemning his wife for her actions. Rev. A. E. Flaxman, preaching at Wombwell Parish Church, conducted one sermon on the theme 'The Wages of Sin is Death'; and Rev. George Hadfield, preaching at Wombwell Congregational Chapel, condemned 'sabbath-breakers, blasphemers, gamblers and adulterers', while expressing sympathy for the defendant because of the 'terrible provocation' he had suffered.

Barnsley Magistrates virtually apologised for having to commit Isaac Hazlehurst for trial on a murder charge rather than manslaughter, the reason being that he did not begin his murderous attack on his wife in the heat of blood. In fact, it seems that the attack started something like three quarters of an hour after he ushered his drinking companions from his home. The magistrates need not have worried, however. The jury took just 25 minutes to clear Isaac Hazlehurst of murder, found him guilty of manslaughter and returned that verdict with a plea for mercy because of the provocation suffered.

Hazlehurst was sentenced to just twelve months hard labour 'to restore his moral calibre', despite his eleven previous convictions for drunkenness, two for gambling, one for causing criminal damage, at least one for poaching and one for assault.

In fairness to Hazlehurst, a well-paid contract miner at Darfield Main, I should say that he also seemed to have a drink problem and that his victim had left him for other men on several occasions in the past.

While being helped by the Salvation Army, he led a blameless life, and his love for his wife always resulted in his seeking her out again or welcoming her back. But when she returned, he always returned to drinking and their life went downhill again. I should also add that Hazlehurst was stricken with grief from the moment he woke up and realised he had murdered his wife and, at one point, cuddled the blood-splattered body. He remained a shadow of his former self, speaking only in monosyllables throughout the duration of the legal proceedings.

Without going into the events leading up to the murder or the grisly events involved, two facts remain worth mentioning. The first is that, although 62 Junction Row was a humble one-up, one-down, back-to-back cottage, it was known that a brand new strong iron bed had been installed there. After the murder, it was found that one of the main side rails was bent almost to the floor. Did Hazlehurst find superhuman strength to bend the bed in his anger at his wife's infidelity, or did she meet her death not just as a result of her sex romp but also because of the damage it caused? We shall never know but a Chronicle reporter of the day seems to have formed his own opinion when he wrote: 'It is impossible to conceive that one man – even raging like a wild animal – could bend the stout iron piece in such a way.'

Secondly, and adding a touch of the macabre, it seems the victim's mother, Mrs Caroline Wraith, may also have been murdered by her husband some twelve years earlier. An inquest on Mrs Caroline Wraith, held at Darfield's Station Inn on December 19th, 1874, produced the following verdict: 'The deceased died of an absess on the brain probably brought on by violence.' Shortly before her death, Mrs Wraith told P.C. Ellis that her head wound had been caused by her husband, George, hitting her with a poker or fender. He maintained that she had been drunk and fell down as he tried to take her home. The evidence was therefore circumstantial and George Wraith, who Mrs Wraith had married bigamously, was never charged with causing her death.

Indeed, he was still alive and able to give evidence at the inquest on his daughter, held at the Guide Post Inn.

Victim: ***Edward G. Copley, shot,*** **April 1887**

Policeman's son David Pilmore certainly killed once – probably twice – and appeared to have got away with it. Having assumed another name he had enlisted in the Royal Berkshire Regiment, and was in the clear – until he spent a night alone on sentry duty. Suddenly, that night he found he wasn't alone. With him was the ghost of a man whose life he had taken almost eight months before when the contents of a shotgun were discharged into his chest from point-blank range.

A short while later, on Christmas Eve, 1887, Cudworth's blackest son was confessing his crimes to a senior officer. The latter listened patiently as Pilmore told him how he and another Cudworth man, Harry Roberts, had set off on a poaching expedition early on the morning of April 29th and met gamekeeper William Illingworth and his assistant Edward George Copley. Pilmore, aged 25 and a former miner, told the truth when he described how Copley, a 30-year-old father-of-two fell to the ground dying a few minutes later. The only fact he changed was his claim that it was Roberts who had fired the fatal shot.

Probably he was also telling the truth when he said that he had 'hastened the end' of his accomplice Roberts, while they were both hiding from the resulting manhunt, in quiet woods near Wakefield some three weeks later, and that he had buried the body.

But the officer didn't believe a word of it and put the amazing confession down to Pilmore's drunken condition. It was only when Pilmore repeated his claims in the sober light of Christmas Day, that the police were informed and Pilmore was arrested.

A short while later Pilmore was on his way from Reading to Pontefract, having been identified as Yorkshire's most wanted criminal by a police officer who had worked with him at a Cudworth Colliery. And so began a fascinating sequence of events which saw Pilmore tried for wilful murder, found guilty and sentenced to death before receiving an eleventh-hour reprieve after 65,000 Yorkshire people signed a petition for leniency.

Before taking a peep at the judicial proceedings, we should, perhaps, examine the events of that fateful morning of April 29th.

Illingworth and Copley were in the employ of Captain R. H. Jones of Badsworth Hall when they came across Pilmore and Roberts shooting at hares on Badsworth Common. Neither Illingworth nor Copley were armed. It appears that the gamekeepers knew the poachers, at least by sight. Their job should have been to ascertain their names and report the matter to the appropriate authorities. Instead of that, Illingworth sent Copley to cover a possible escape route while he followed the poachers. They initially promised to go away if left alone, but Illingworth continued to follow them. That resulted in Pilmore twice levelling a double-barrelled shotgun at him and making threats to put a hole through him.

When the poachers broke into a run near some railway lines, Illingworth gave chase. The poachers stopped running and stood their ground. Roberts, the elder of the two, described to Barnsley Magistrates as 'the pest of Cudworth' earlier the same year – seized a stake and attacked Illingworth with it.

Illingworth, having shouted to Copley to assist him, used Roberts as a shield as Pilmore levelled his gun for a third time. Then Copley appeared, rushing at Pilmore. The gun went off and Copley collapsed at Pilmore's feet. Illingworth had dealt some sturdy blows to Roberts with his stick but was dragged to the ground. He was then bludgeoned with the gun-stock and, on his evidence, left for dead.

In fact he recovered in minutes but Copley had no chance of life. He died on the Saturday evening having given his evidence to the police in 'the expectation and belief of approaching death' – he never lost consciousness until the end.

The surgeon who pulled 68 pellets, not to mention several pieces of clothing, out of a fist-sized hole in his chest during a subsequent post mortem examination was amazed that he had lived so long.

Pilmore and Roberts returned to the latter's lodgings with Mary Childs at Sidcop, Cudworth, later the same morning. They said nothing about the morning's events and left separately after Roberts had had treatment for head wounds and both had eaten breakfast. Pilmore was not seen again until his dramatic Christmas confession. Roberts, as far as is known, was never ever seen again.

Pilmore did not persist in his story that Roberts had fired the shot which killed Copley when he faced trial at Leeds Assizes on February 21st. His main defence was that he should not have been charged with murder, but manslaughter.

Through his counsel, Mr C. Mellor, he claimed that the gun had gone off accidentally, possibly triggered by Copley's run at him. Mr Mellor told the jury that all they, as poachers, were required to do by law was tender their names. They had not, in fact, been asked their names but they had offered to leave the area peacefully. The gamekeepers' overreaction, he added, should automatically have reduced the charge to manslaughter.

That defence didn't find much favour with the jury. They took just 20 minutes to return a verdict of guilty. Nor did it appear to sway Mr Justice Day who passed the death sentence, with an appeal for Pilmore to seek mercy at the feet of his Saviour. But it did persuade many people – not least the *Barnsley Chronicle* which had previously published letters, sent by Pilmore to his father, which pleaded his innocence of murder and saying that the killing was accidental.

In one of those letters Pilmore damned Illingworth for lying at the trial and predicted a petition to the Home Secretary as 'all time and trouble thrown away'. He predicted wrongly. A petition document was made available for public signatures at the Chronicle's Peel

Square offices on Friday. By the following Tuesday the list of names was 120 feet long. In all 66,735 Yorkshire people added their names to the petition for mercy in less than five days. It's difficult to say why Pilmore's plight aroused such sympathy. By his own admission he had enjoyed a 'wild and dissolute career', despite his good family background. He had also served six months in prison in connection with a poaching affray at Oulton Park, Leeds, five years before.

Certainly The *Barnsley Chronicle* newspaper did not consider that malice aforethought had been proved against him and pointed out that the trial judge had 'contrary to custom', allowed Illingworth to listen to the case before giving his evidence. When he took the stand, therefore, he knew exactly what his evidence had to prove.

But in the face of such public opinion the Home Secretary, Mr Henry Matthews Q.C., did grant a reprieve just hours before Pilmore was due to climb the gallows on March 13th, 1888. The death sentence was replaced by one of penal servitude for life.

That leaves us with one mystery remaining — what happened to the 'pest' of Cudworth? Was Harry Roberts so weak from his head wounds and three weeks of living rough without food that Pilmore did hasten his end? Or was Pilmore trying to end the search for his partner in crime? We shall never know. Pilmore was released in July 1898.

Victim: ***John Taylor, knifed,* June 1887**

William Teale must rank as Barnsley's most unlikely killer. The colliery clerk and secretary of Ardsley's Conservative Club was just five feet in height and of very weak build. It was probably because of lack of size and strength that he was frightened, particularly of passing through Measbrough Dyke which in 1887, was a hamlet half in Barnsley and half in Ardsley. Many times, the quiet 30-year-old chose the longer route through Hoyle Mill to get from Barnsley to his Ardsley home, rather than risk trouble by passing through the hamlet.

Unfortunately, he didn't take that decision on the night of Saturday, June 25. Perhaps influenced by drink, he decided to be brave. The result was death – not his own but that of 19-year-old colliery trammer John Taylor.

Prior to that night there is no evidence to suggest the two had ever laid eyes on each other, but their brief and fateful encounter resulted in Taylor's lifeblood spurting rather than ebbing away from a hole in his jugular vein. Teale himself was caught within seconds of striking the deadly blow with his pocket knife. He was originally charged with murder, but eventually stood trial for manslaughter.

And his belief that Measbrough Dyke was a 'thrashing place', for unwary travellers was to help him receive, what was then, a very lenient sentence for someone having taken human life. Three months' imprisonment with hard labour.

That day of June 25th started innocently enough for Teale, employed as a clerk and rent collector for Mr Charles Cammell and Co's New Oaks Collieries. He went with a team of Ardsley cricketers by wagonette to play a match at Brierley. But Teale finished up at Barnsley's Saturday night market, where he appears to have drunk enough to make him unsteady on his feet. He was walking home to Ardsley, in the company of a friend, when he came across four Measbrough Dyke youths named as John Clarke, Thomas Woodward, Herbert Brown and Ernest Walton. One of the youths knew Teale's companion and addressed him by his nickname, Poppy, and that seems to have annoyed Teale. He walked over to the group and told them: 'Dost tha know that when tha calls my friend, tha also call me'.

The youths ran off, but Teale again approached them when they stopped to break open a coconut in Doncaster Road. Teale then punched Clarke in the face and threatened to kick them. Although Clarke was crying, his friends were less concerned. At least one of them told Teale he 'wouldn't have thing all his own road' when he reached 'the Dyke'. Teale, then seen to have a pocket knife in his possession, said words to the effect that he would be prepared.

Fear was now setting in. Teale became separated from Poppy and, a short time later, was heard saying to another man, identified only as 'Norman': 'Are you going to see me slogged at the Dyke with a lot of men yonder'. Despite that plea for help, Teale was alone when he reached a group of men standing outside the Pindar Oaks public house. Two of the four youths he had had the earlier altercation with were behind him, the other two are believed to have run ahead and told the men what had transpired.

Teale was in the roadway, his eyes downcast and little legs striding quickly when Taylor seized hold of him, presumably to ask for an explanation of the attack on young Clarke. Harry Ellis, a miner at Pindar Oaks Colliery, told a later inquest that the two presented a comical picture as they held one another and that he was laughing – he didn't laugh long.

Taylor's only word, 'Hello', was followed by 'Leave go' from Teale, closely followed by what, at first, appeared to be a punch. Taylor then stood back and said: 'Fetch a doctor, Tubber – he's stabbed me', as the blood started spurting from his neck. Those words were the last he spoke. Thirty minutes later the young knur and spell exponent had bled to death. A trail of blood showed the path taken as he tried to walk to his home at Middle Row, Pindar Oaks Terrace. He didn't make it, and had to be carried into the house where he died a short while later after losing consciousness.

Teale tried to run off after striking the deadly blow, but had only got about 50 yards before he fell. Seized roughly by a group of men demanding to know where the knife was, he replied: 'I have not gone one'. The knife, an innocuous-looking weapon with a bigger corkscrew than blade, was later found nearby and identified as the one used by Teale to make erasures from his colliery books.

The following day saw Measbrough Dyke

visited by hundreds of people determined to view the bloodstains, and Monday saw Barnsley Magistrates' Court packed as Teale, 'looking bewildered and frightened', was charged with wilful murder. Teale was also present when the inquest was held in the Pindar Oaks public house, and heard the coroner state that, if Taylor had known he was carrying a knife, he could be considered in some respects the author of his own misfortune.

It took the jury 30 minutes – a long time by the standards of those days – to come back with a manslaughter rather than guilty verdict. Most of those present then left the inquest to join the funeral procession as it went past the pub on its way to Barnsley Cemetery. Teale's second appearance before the Magistrates saw the charge reduced to one of manslaughter. He was granted bail in the sum of £100 for himself and £50 each from father and brother-in-law.

In early August, Teale pleaded not guilty to feloniously killing and slaying John Taylor at the West Riding Assize hearing before Mr Justice Mathew at Leeds. His defence was simple. It was that he was 'half drunk' and desperately wanting to get past a group of men at what he believed was a noted 'thrashing place'. When seized by one of the men he tried to struggle free, then struck out without being mentally aware that he had an open pocket knife in his hand. The jury were not convinced and returned a guilty verdict, but with a recommendation for mercy because of 'provocation'.

The judge agreed that Teale had been greatly provoked and said the three months hard labour was intended as a 'short, sharp lesson' to Teale and that he hoped he would spend the time redeeming his character.

Whether Teale did redeem his character is not known. He became famous in the township because of one wild swing with a pocket knife never intended to have the tragic consequences it did have, and seems to have faded back into obscurity almost as quickly. In one respect, he was perhaps lucky. Three months' hard labour is not a long sentence for someone who has taken a human life. On the other hand, he was unlucky. He had to spend the rest of his life knowing he was a killer.

No doubt he went to his death wondering how such a small wound – half-an-inch across and one-and-a-half inches deep – could have had such a catastrophic effect. Almost any other part of the human body would have resulted in Taylor's being hurt, but not killed; but a direct hit on the jugular vein robbed young John Taylor of any chance of realising full maturity.

Victim: ***Aileen Ethel Oone Burke,*** **February 1888**

Shortly after 9 p.m. on Saturday, February 4th, 1888, a little girl – often called Topsy Chatterbox – was roused from her slumbers. She thought she was going to Barnsley to see a pantomime: in reality, she had a date with death. Less than two hours later, eight year old Aileen Ethel Oone Burke lay dead on the floor of a Monk Bretton public house. A bullet had passed through her heart and lung and lodged in her back. Standing beside her was the father who had dubbed her Topsy Chatterbox, Dr William Henry Emeris Burke, his waistcoat was on fire and blood was pouring from a chest wound. After shooting his daughter at point-blank range, he had turned the gun on himself. But the wound was not to prove fatal. He was to recover, face trial and be sentenced to death... before an eleventh hour reprieve.

He didn't know it, but it was that reprieve that was the cause of a furore in the town – the reason being that a young Barnsley brickworks labourer was not destined to be so fortunate. His hanging was to bring the public of Barnsley out on to the streets to protest about there being one law for the middle classes and another for the working class.

News of this grisly murder in the best room of the Norman Inn, Monk Bretton, was first announced in a special edition of the *Barnsley Chronicle* produced on Monday, February 6th. Staff worked day and night almost from the time of the murder to

The Norman Inn, Monk Bretton, where the tragedy took place.

produce a four-page supplement sold for a halfpenny.

They reported how Dr Burke had doted on his 'pretty, dark haired, rosy faced girl – the very picture of health and childish beauty'. They also reported how she kept her looks in death and how her 'calm face was like a picture'. As prosecution counsel were to echo later, 'The only good thing that could be said about the terrible deed was that death was painless and the little girl died without tasting illness or fear – loved and loving'.

To precis the facts of the case, we should say that Emeris Burke was of Irish parentage. Some reports say he was a solicitor's son, others that he was the offspring of an Irish Priest converted to the Protestant faith. We do know for fact that his elder half-brother, the Vicar of Plumpton-Wall, had been curate to the Rev. A. Lambert at Monk Bretton some 15 years earlier.

Dr Burke appears to have arrived in Monk Bretton around the same time as his brother, met Mr Lambert's daughter Katherine Jane and fallen in love. They had two children by their marriage, Aileen and a boy, named George Hewlett Burke in some accounts and Hubert Evelyn Ulrick Burke in others. Two other children had died in infancy.

Dr Burke was known as a skilful and careful practitioner in his duties as surgeon to the Monk Bretton, Carlton Main and Monckton Main Collieries, but his affinity for drink had resulted in the dwindling of his private practices at Monk Bretton and Cudworth. Shortly before the tragedy, Dr Burke had been working for a medical practitioner named Smith in Barnsley. That affinity for drink had also resulted in an unhappy marriage and Mrs Burke had left him on several occasions. Ironically she and the children had returned to him just two weeks before the murder took place.

On that day Dr Burke had spent most of his time drinking in the Norman Inn before going home to collect his wife and 'little girlie'.

The horse and carriage, driven by the village blacksmith, was requested to stop outside the Norman Inn just for a minute, but the doctor later returned and asked his wife and the girl to accompany him inside to the otherwise empty best room. There they stayed drinking port and champagne until just before closing time at 11 p.m.

Then Mrs Burke ran from the room screaming.

Spotting Police Constable Francis Emslie in the other room, she cried: 'He's got that nasty pistol in his pocket – go take it from him.' From that point, accounts of the murder differ. Mrs Burke told the inquest, held in the Pheasant Inn, Monk Bretton, that P.C. Emslie

Above: Interior of the Norman Inn where little Topsy Chatterbox was shot by her father.
Right: The murderer, Dr William Burke.

ignored her pleas and her accusations of cowardice until after the shots were fired.

P.C. Emslie, on the other hand, said the 'coward' taunt was delivered in presumption that he would not respond. He told both the committal hearing before Barnsley Magistrates and Leeds Assize Court, before Mr Justice Matthew, that he opened the door of the best room just in time to see Dr Burke aim and fire the pistol at his daughter and then turn the gun on himself.

The law of the land at that time stated that a wife could not give evidence at her husband's trial, even if that evidence was in his defence. The jury who tried the case, therefore, had no evidence before them other than that he deliberately pointed his gun at his defenceless and dutiful daughter and fired.

Dr Burke's defence – that the revolver was discharged accidentally – seemed bound to fail from the outset, but that wasn't the only damning evidence against him. The other was a letter from him to Mrs Burke which he had written earlier that evening.

The letter, obtained from Mrs Burke by Police Superintendent Kane shortly after the shooting, said that he had loved her hard, but that his love had been converted to entire indifference by her actions of running away from him. It also said that he now loved Mary Anne Taylor, nee Woodcock, but that she preferred a clandestine relationship and had discarded a more formal proposition.

While containing no mention of suicide, those words accompanied by 'Last to K.' written on the envelope, were judged to having indicated his intention of self destruction if not the killing of his daughter.

Controversy raged about whether Supt. Kane had the authority to take that letter from Mrs Burke. And that controversy, coupled with

The Manor House, Monk Bretton, home of the Burkes.

Mrs Burke being denied the right to give evidence, was perhaps instrumental in the death sentence being commuted to one of penal servitude just two days before his scheduled execution. Also helpful was a petition, available for signing at the Chronicle office and several public houses, which attracted over 9,000 signatures.

As it happened, the doctor didn't live long and many people were far from upset at his passing. They had never understood how a 'drunkard and debauchee', who had strongly condemned William Murphy and David Pilmore for their killings, should escape the noose, whereas a clean living brickworks labourer whose crime we shall be looking at next, didn't.

If the truth be known, the doctor had been fortunate to recover from his own self inflicted wound. While he remained conscious after the shooting, and even asked to kiss his daughter before she was taken home to Monk Bretton's Manor House, he was soon fighting for his life in Barnsley's Beckett Hospital. The bullet had missed his lung but had passed through the chest cavity. A recent attack of pleurisy and the ravages of drink combined to make his recovery slow and irregular. For some of that time Emeris Burke was rambling – his mind adrift. One wonders today whether he would ever be called to face trial, or if a plea of temporary insanity would be accepted.

In those days, however, such temporary insanity was put down to drink, and the abolitionists were quick to point out that drunkenness could never mitigate murder... certainly not the murder of little Topsy Chatterbox.

Victim: ***William Berridge, shot,*** **March 1888**

James William Richardson was a cold-blooded killer and many people believed he should hang. He did. On April 22th, 1888, he met the most fearsome form of judicial punishment at the age of 23. In doing so, he is believed to have made history as the first man to have a jury's plea for mercy completely disregarded. His death certainly caused a furore about British justice that took years to die down.

The furore was caused by the fact that Richardson's murder of his foreman, although cowardly and indefensible, was perhaps less vile than the murder committed by Dr Burke – the subject of the previous profile.

In Richardson's case, the jury unanimously recommended that mercy should be shown. No such plea by the jury was delivered in the case of Dr Burke who callously shot his own daughter through the heart.

Yet Richardson, a young man of previous good character, was executed, while Dr Burke, described by one leading clergyman as a 'drunkard and debauchee', had had his sentence commuted to one of penal servitude for life. Not surprisingly the public of Barnsley were furious. Radicals, Liberals, Tories, rich men, poor men, the high and the low, all complained that the Home Secretary's decision had proved there was one law for the rich and another for the poor.

Before examining that public outcry we should perhaps, have a look at the crime itself.

Richardson and William Berridge (often spelled Burridge) were both employed at Messrs H. and F. Chamberlain's Brick and Carbon Works in Dodworth Road, Barnsley. Richardson, married with a daughter just a few months old, had worked there for five years, originally as a brickworks labourer, before joining the carbon department which produced carbons for electric lighting. Berridge, a 36-year-old father of four, who lived in Eldon Terrace, Dodworth Road, was his foreman and had been employed there around 15 years. Both men were generally well liked, but Richardson was described by workmates as a 'passionable' individual.

On Wednesday, February 21st, 1888, the two men were seen to argue on two separate occasions. The noise of the machinery drowned their words but, after the last occasion, Richardson threw down his brush, picked up his coat and went home.

He breakfasted at home, told his wife he had been discharged, washed, changed and set off back to work to collect his money and 'finish up'. At 11.30 that morning he was outside the works office asking to see co-owner, Mr Francis Chamberlain. The latter was in the company of Berridge who, after a few minutes, walked out of the office apparently without noticing Richardson.

Suddenly a shot rang out. Mr Chamberlain and a young office boy turned round to see Richardson standing behind Berridge, a revolver in his hand. As Berridge crumpled to the floor, at least two more shots were fired. Richardson started to run off, but stopped when Mr Chamberlain called out: 'What have you done this for?' His answer was that he either was, or must have been, mad.

He duly surrendered himself to Mr Chamberlain and, still with revolver in pocket, walked to Barnsley's Westgate police station.

Berridge lived for a further nine days at Barnsley's Beckett Hospital, but his case was hopeless from the start. A bullet had entered his brain just in front of his ear and another had penetrated his back. Sometimes he tried to speak but he always failed.

Surrounded by his family, he died on Sunday, April 1. Family, friends, workmates and fellow members of the Ancient Order of Foresters attended his funeral on the Thursday at Pitt Street Wesleyan Chapel, before interment in Barnsley Cemetery.

The prosecution case, put to Mr Justice Mathew at Leeds Assizes on May 3rd, was that Richardson had returned home for the gun and deliberately wreaked the ultimate vengeance on Berridge for dismissing him.

The case for the defence was that Richardson had returned to the works only to collect his money. He had found the revolver in his pocket en route, having previously cleaned it with the intention of pawning it to raise money.

He had not envisaged seeing Berridge on his return and nothing untoward would have taken place had not Berridge 'sneered and hissed' at him and jostled him in the ribs with his elbow. Thus provoked, he grasped the gun and fired in a rage at Berridge's middle portions – the fatal head wound being sustained as Berridge fell to the floor.

Richardson, newspaper reports said, had maintained a 'stolid and

Supplement to the Barnsley Chronicle

[GRATIS.] BARNSLEY, SATURDAY, MARCH 31, 1888. [GRATIS.]

THE DODWORTH ROAD TRAGEDY, MARCH 21st, 1888.

Beckett Hospital and Dispensary.

The Revolver.

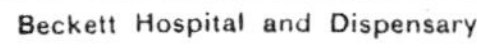

James William Richardson.

Scene of the Tragedy.

General View of Messrs. Chamberlain's Brick and Carbon Works.

Lingard, Litho., Barnsley.]

[From Photographs by J. Walker & Son, Barnsley.

A special supplement to the Barnsley Chronicle, March 31, 1888.

callous demeanour' when before Barnsley Magistrates for committal proceedings, but that ended when he gave his evidence. He gave his evidence in a 'broken piteous voice which at times was almost a wail', and the jury appeared 'touched by the unutterable woe and despair of his trembling account — some of them cried'.

Sobbing bitterly, Richardson concluded: 'God help me – God help him'.

Richardson was one of four prisoners sentenced to death for wilful murder at that Assize session. All the others had their sentences commuted. The last to have his sentence commuted was Dr Burke. He had to wait until two days before he, like Richardson, was to climb the gallows. A petition for a reprieve had been started in respect of both men. Nine thousand people from all over Yorkshire signed that for Dr Burke, 8,400 from Barnsley and Leeds alone signed that for Richardson, but it was only after Dr Burke's reprieve that things really started to happen.

On Whitsuntide Monday – the day before the execution – speaker after speaker addressed a massive public meeting in Peel Square to protest at the different treatment of the two men. Among letters read to the meeting was one from a juror at Richardson's trial, who said that if he had had any idea that their recommendation for mercy wouldn't have earned a respite, then he would not have agreed to anything but manslaughter.

The meeting decided to send Richardson's father and a Barnsley gentleman to the Home Office that night. They were to point out the jury's plea, and that Richardson was little more than a boy with boyish passions, was of good character and from a good family, with a good work record. The deputation failed. Notified of the failure by wire, over 5,000 people attended a second meeting in Peel Square at 10 p.m. on the eve of the execution. Clergyman appealed to the crowd not to engage in public disorder, while lambasting the Mayor for not supporting the cause.

Richardson's father and the gentleman arrived in Penistone, via Manchester, at 3 a.m. Unable to afford 18s for a carriage, they then had to walk to Barnsley. Mr Richardson collapsed exhausted when he sighted his son's cottage at the Keresforth Road entrance to Locke Park.

Two hours later, at 8 a.m., his youngest son was dead. All that remained of him were letters, published in the *Barnsley Chronicle*, thanking everyone for their efforts on his behalf and adding: 'May God help the wife and children of poor Berridge and bring them safely through life'.

The Chronicle appeared to have mixed feelings on the events of the day. One report said: 'Strange yet true it is, he gained the respect of all who came into contact with him in gaol, and some of the wardens were more moved than he in preparing for the execution and burial'.

Another said: 'Six cowardly and brutal homicides in less than two years brought too much shame and disgrace on the Barnsley District', and considered whether the Home Secretary had to make an example of someone to show that such acts would not be tolerated.

Foremost in the condemnation of the Home Secretary were the clergymen, with Rev. W. Dawkins, of Blucher Street's Methodist Free Church, leading the attack. Local M.P. Mr Courtney Kenny also demanded that the Home Secretary should explain to the Commons why he chose to spare one man the gallows and not another, ignoring jury recommendations. Above all, it seemed that a jury's power had been devalued, and the controversy might have lasted for years had it not been for one thing – Dr Burke's death.

The public of Barnsley were convinced that the Lord had meted out his own justice to prove that, in his eyes, all men were equal.

Victim: ***Margaret Hill, shot,*** **September 1888**

Margaret Hill died in agony at the age of 22, after receiving two blasts from a shotgun at point blank range. The servant girl sank to her knees in an upstairs room of the Blacksmiths Arms, Millhouse Green, Penistone. She had just two hours to live – as had her unborn child.

It was September 3rd, 1888, a date marking the demise of one of Barnsley's most unfortunate murder victims. 'Unfortunate' is an adjective that could be used to describe Maggie Hill's entire life. The daughter of a Bullhouse labourer, she became a mother to two illegitimate children early in life. Her marriage to the father of those children was arranged but never took place – he died shortly before the appointed day.

And 'unfortunate', can certainly be used to describe Maggie Hill's death. She was shot by her innkeeper employer, Henry Hey, not because she had done anything to displease him, but because he was suffering delusions caused by temporary insanity. All through the previous night 35-year-old Hey, a plasterer who had turned his hand to innkeeping two years before, had wandered from room to room upstairs and downstairs with gun in hand, ready to do battle with imaginary people he believed were out to kill him.

Just a few minutes before the shooting, Hey, his gun trained above Maggie's head, had been joined in the upstairs room by his 13-year-old son Ben.

The latter, hearing his father say such things as, 'You wouldn't shoot me in front of my son – would you kill Sam?', tried to take the weapon from him. Unfortunately he failed, his father protesting: 'No, don't take my gun – take his or he'll kill me', while gesticulating at the invisible Sam. Implored by his trembling and shaking father and by Maggie to leave the room, the lad returned downstairs.

Moments later the two shots were heard and the lad returned to hear his father say, 'Oh Ben – I've shot Maggie. I didn't do it on purpose, I thought it was somebody else.'

The gunshots, fired at 9 a.m., shook the inhabitants of Millhouse

Green who gathered outside frightened to enter. It was only after Hey himself smashed the window and implored them to come upstairs that a group of men entered. They found Maggie Hill bleeding badly, in great pain and not wishing to be moved to the nearby bed. At one point she pleaded with them to give her something to 'finish' her.

Hey was rambling incoherently, saying at one point that she had betrayed him and, at another, that he had shot his best friend. He also told them that he intended to 'do her' and then turn the gun on himself, but the first shot only hit her arm. He then fired the second shot, but didn't have another cartridge left for himself.

Not surprisingly, there was great interest in the crime locally.

The *Barnsley Chronicle* helped stir that interest with the dramatic announcement that it was 'a record of sorrow, trouble, passion and debauchery – a story of weak yielding to appetite, of

Blacksmiths Arms, Millhouse Green where a servant girl and her unborn child met a violent death.

desires indulged, of passion unchecked leading to strife, sorrow and trouble to shame, delirium and death'.

Three hours and 40 minutes after the murder, a large crowd had assembled at Barnsley railway station to see the accused, but it was disappointed. Hey and his police escort got off the train near Summer Lane and walked to Westgate Police Station. Hey's appearance in court later that afternoon shocked the people there, he was described as 'jaunty, bright-eyed and with a face flushed with excitement'. But a week later at the committal proceedings, he appeared 'sorrowful and stricken'.

The court was hushed as witnesses told how Hey, a father of five sons and one daughter, was normally well-liked, genial and respected. He often employed others to work for him as a plasterer, was a good boss and a well-respected brass band musician, both at Thurlstone and Barnsley. The exception was when he was in drink, when his behaviour was much less agreeable. Taking over the Blacksmiths Arms had, of course, presented him with the opportunity of taking strong drink whenever he wanted. As a result, his marriage had suffered and his wife, Elizabeth, had left him on several occasions.

Hey had in fact appeared before Barnsley Magistrates in March that year, charged with assaulting his wife and a woman neighbour. The charge relating to his wife was dropped, but Hey was fined 20s and costs for assaulting the neighbour. Mrs Hey, interestingly enough, had run from the public house to seek refuge with neighbours early on the day of the murder. She knew that Hey had received medical treatment for delirium tremens on several previous occasions and was afraid to be near when she saw another fit coming over him. She also claimed that she had told Maggie Hill to take a similar course of action, although she admitted she was jealous of her, 'and had good reason to be so'. The fact that Maggie Hill was four months pregnant may explain the latter remark.

The jury at Leeds Assizes, presided over by Baron Pollock, heard a lot more about Hey's state of mind at the time of the offence. Young Ben Hey told them how his father believed the house was besieged by cats. And the arresting police officer, Catherall, told them how Hey told him that there were cats in the drains and a regiment of soldiers waiting to shoot them as they walked to Penistone police station immediately after the arrest.

They also heard of his strange reply after being charged with murder, 'Well I don't know – I have a bad wife'. The jury also heard Wakefield prison's medical officer, Dr Henry Clarke, and Dr Bevan

Lewis of the West Riding Lunatic Asylum, say that identity problems and delusions were classic symptoms of delirium tremens – the dilated pupils, general muscular tremor and profuse perspiration being difficult to feign.

Without hearing evidence for the defence, they returned a verdict that Henry, often called Harry Hey, was guilty of wilful murder but while in a state of unsound mind. He was ordered to be detained until Her Majesty's Pleasure be known.

What the jury didn't know was that Henry Hey had already made his peace with his victim. In the time between those fateful shots and being led away 75 minutes later, he had begged forgiveness and a kiss. Margaret Hill, despite her agony, had granted both. Forty-five minutes later the unfortunate girl breathed her last in the arms of her parents, after begging them for forgiveness.

Victim: ***Earnest Guest, shot,*** **November 1890**

Ernest Guest was 14 when he first handled a revolver – seconds later he was dead. The seven chambered Colt was little more than a toy, firing a tiny size .230 pellet; but a bullet in the brain from point blank range ensured his death. It also resulted in 17 year old Alfred Ogley facing the most frightening few days of his life, and a public outcry about the ease with which young people could lay their hands on firearms.

That outcry in November 1890, was led by the *Barnsley Chronicle*, who said it hoped the publicity given to young Guest's death would have some effect in checking the 'revolver mania which appears to be manifesting itself to an alarming extent among a section of the youth of Barnsley'. The editorial continued: 'When lads in their teens are found to be not merely in possession of revolvers but making arrangements for duels, it is high time that some energetic steps be taken to stamp out the epidemic.'

In truth no duel ever took place – but it nearly did. And one of the parties involved was the same Alfred Ogley, who admitted his hands were on the revolver when Guest received his fatal wound. That fact could have weighed heavily against Ogley, had it not been for Mr Taylor who was coroner at Guest's inquest. Several of the jurors attached great significance to evidence they had heard about Ogley being a party to a cancelled duel. They bombarded him with questions about the duel and why he had the revolver in his possession, but Mr Taylor ruled both lines of questioning illegal.

Questions about the duel he said, were inadmissable because Guest was not the other party to the duel and questions about why he had a gun in his possession were out of order because, if Ogley intended to shoot someone other than Guest, the evidence could incriminate him.

The exchanges between coroner and jurors were heated and angry, and the Chronicle sided with the jurors and publicly criticised Mr Taylor for ruling some of the questions out of order.

Blaming 'Dick Turpin' and 'Claude DuVal' literature for firing the youth of Barnsley with romantic ideas about guns, the Chronicle called for Barnsley to have its own coroner, stating that an area stretching from Bradford to Wortley was much too large for one coroner to have jurisdiction over. The Chronicle also stated what it knew about the duel. Without naming Ogley as being involved, the paper said that two youths agreed to fight a duel at the Dodworth Road tip, before changing the venue to Greenfoot Lane. Stating that there was 'silly braggadocio' over the affair, it claimed that the only reason the duel did not take place was because one party arrived without a gun. Fisticuffs were suggested as an alternative, but that required 'too much pluck' and was not sufficiently dignified, so the event was postponed. The Chronicle concluded that while the

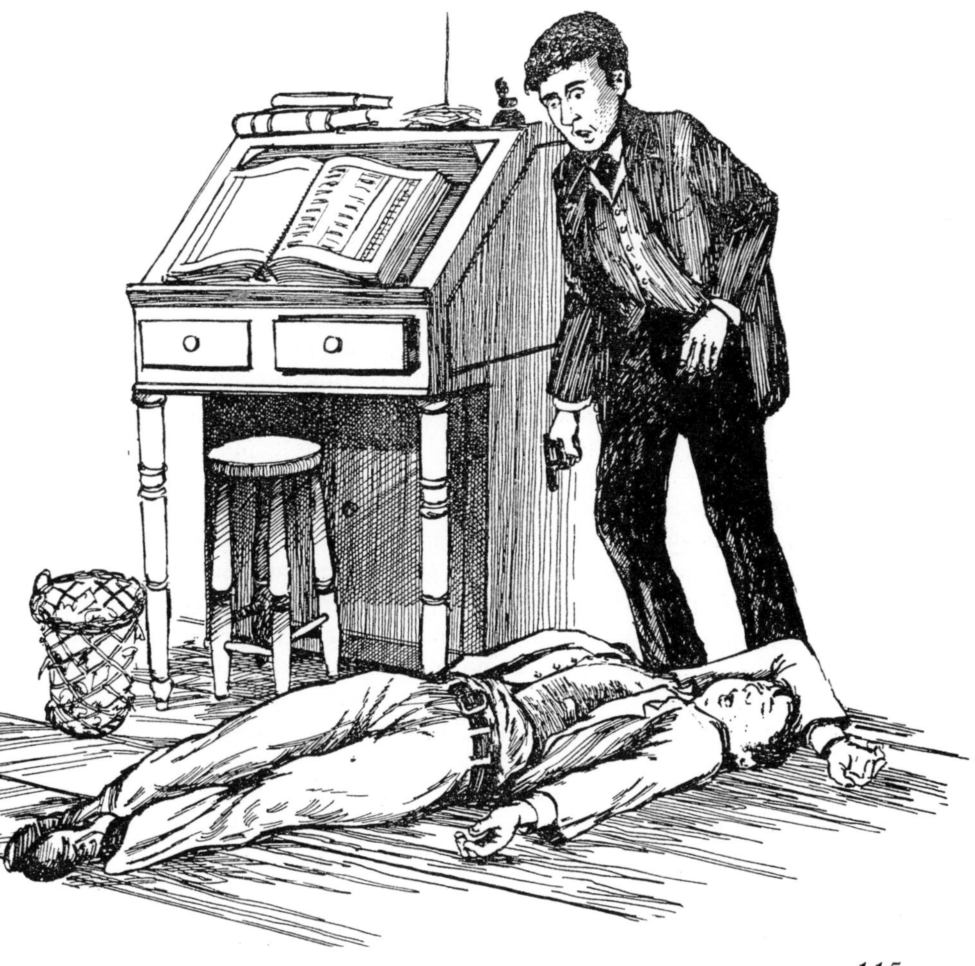

principals described the event as a 'mock duel', their seconds admitted they were genuinely frightened.

Before looking at the inquest in closer detail, we should first look at the circumstances of Guest's death.

Ernest Guest, the 'fine, strong son', of Shambles Street butcher Mr William Guest and Ogley, the son of a recently-deceased journeyman printer, were both employed by Messrs. R. Craik and Co., East Gawber Collieries. Ogley was employed at the firm's Church Street office, where the College of Technology now stands. Guest worked from the company's Pontefract Road depot.

At about 2.45 p.m. Guest arrived at the Church Street office to find Ogley alone. Ogley showed him the revolver he had borrowed from a youth called Harry Gardham, who lived in Lancaster Street.

The revolver had just one bullet in it.

Ogley became worried about how the gun was being handled, walked over to Guest, who was sitting on a high stool, and pointed the barrel upwards. At that moment Guest appeared to slip from the stool. His head went forward and the revolver went off. The ball shaped pellet entered his head just above the right eye and lodged in the brain. Horrified at what had happened, Ogley fled outside, where he met two 16 year olds: William Thomas, a butcher's boy of Lancaster Street and Thomas Garner, an apprentice whitesmith with Messrs Lowrance and Sons, who lived in Alma Street. They went to the home of Ogley's aunt who lived opposite, and then to inform Dr Lancaster, before Thomas and Garner recruited passers-by to help them carry the unconscious Guest to Barnsley Beckett Hospital, where he died the following Sunday night.

Ogley was placed in the cells after giving a statement to the police, but was soon released on bail. The Chronicle, unfortunately fails to inform us with what offence he was charged with. It was young Thomas Garner who told the stormy inquest that several youths in the area possessed guns – and about the postponed duel.

He also discredited Ogley's evidence that he had only borrowed the gun the previous night: he said Ogley had produced it to a number of youths gathered at Town End on the Sunday. Finally, both Garner and Thomas swore that Ogley emerged into Church Street from his office shouting, 'I've shot Guest – what shall I do?' Ogley maintained he said: 'Guest's been shot – what shall I do?'

Ogley's own account to the inquest was somewhat different from that given to the police, when he said the revolver's contents were discharged as it was being 'passed' back. He told the inquest Guest had triggered the gun on its empty chambers while pointing it about the office. He then turned round to find Guest levelling the gun at his back so immediately went to take the gun from him. 'He was only doing it for a lark,' added Ogley, 'but could have shot me with the next barrel.'

The jury unanimously returned a verdict of accidental death, but many people, including Guest's father and some members of the jury were not altogether convinced by Ogley's account and were far from happy about the way the inquest was conducted. Nobody ever suggested that Guest's death was anything other than an accident. The questions to be asked were: was Guest really the agent of his own misfortune? Or could it have been, that it was Ogley who was larking around with the gun and Guest who paid the price?

Either way the public of Barnsley became very concerned about the 'revolver epidemic', so much so that the jury had considered adding a statement to their verdict. However they decided not to add the statement saying, 'We think Parliament will not take much notice of twelve jurors from Barnsley so we will leave that to bigger men to say something'.

No doubt the public's concern was heightened by the fact that guns had figured greatly in Barnsley's darkest deeds of the previous three years: Pilmore had killed a gamekeeper in 1887, Dr Burke had used a gun to murder his young daughter, Richardson had used a gun to slay his foreman and innkeeper Henry Hey had used a gun to kill his maidservant.

The inquest on Guest was not only stormy because of questions being ruled out of order by the coroner. Half way through the afternoon a juror named Lockwood started asking questions about the length of the trial and the number of witnesses to be called.

After receiving 'don't know' answers, Mr Lockwood rose to his feet, announced that he had breakfasted before 7 a.m. and was going for his dinner. 'I may be back in an hour,' he added.

The coroner immediately ordered: 'Stop that man – such nonsense. Bring him back in custody'. He then told Lockwood he must not leave the room. Having been told that the Law demanded his continued attendance, Lockwood said:

'Then you will have to get me some refreshment in the room – I'm not going to perish for all the coroners in the world. I asked two or three reasonable questions and couldn't get a civil answer.'

Mr Lockwood, I'm afraid didn't get his meal. He did, however, get an assurance from the coroner that a doctor at the hearing would give him a stimulant if he felt likely to faint.

Victim: ***Charles Braithwaite, poisoned,*** **June 1891**

Little Charles Braithwaite was just 17 months old when he became a murder victim on June 29th, 1891. He died with a stomach full of laudanum administered by his mother, but as a judge later pointed out, Charles Braithwaite was a victim of 'red tapeism' which allowed his mother, 35 year old Mary Braithwaite, out of a lunatic asylum on a technicality.

She should have been re-certified and returned to Wadsley Asylum, but she wasn't. The result was that Charles died while his three year old sister, Alice, was fortunate to survive and public concern was so great that questions were asked in Parliament. To examine this outcry it may be best if we go right back to the beginning and follow the events chronologically.

Mary Braithwaite, nee Depledge, was a member of a large family who lived in Silkstone and also for some time, in Dodworth. Her mother died in childbirth when Mary was still fairly young and her father later remarried and moved to Oldham in Lancashire. Mary was about 20 when she married Charles Braithwaite and, at the time of the offence, they were living in Cresswell Street, Pogmoor. The couple had seven children born to them before the arrival of Charles Jnr., but three had died in infancy.

Along with the rigours of looking after such a family and suffering from an ever worsening skin complaint which some people took to be scurvy and others leprosy, but which was more likely to have been psoriasis, Mary Braithwaite also had a job as a hawker from a van, in the employ of general dealer Mr H. Davidson. As such, she was well known throughout the Barnsley area.

All that changed however, when young Charles arrived on the scene. The pregnancy was difficult as was the birth. Mary was left too weak even to suckle the child and was bedfast for several weeks. Dr Macphail originally tended to her needs, but later ended his treatment, saying 'kitchen medicine' was needed. Whatever kitchen medicine was it doesn't seem to have helped, for in September 1890

Mary Braithwaite made an unsuccessful attempt to slash her throat with her husband's razor. She was committed to Wadsley Asylum by Dr John Blackburn after she had told him that her husband and children 'are lost' and that she was determined to 'make away' with herself. But three weeks later she was discharged from the asylum and sent home, where she spent the next eight months as a 'passenger' in the household, being cared for by her husband and children.

So it was that, early on Monday, June 29, Mary set off with Charles in her arms and Alice walking by her side, while her husband, a miner, was at work and the other children were asleep in bed.

Lunchtime saw the trio at Brumley Bridge over the Barnsley Canal at Barugh, when a certain Mary Ellen Burke noticed that the clothes of one of the children were wet. The next time they were seen was around 5 p.m. at Huckset Wood between Dodworth and Silkstone, when Mary flagged down the cart of Silkstone colliery banksman Edmund Taylor and asked him to fetch her sister.

Mr Taylor returned with Mary's sister, Mrs Ada Dyson, to find her and both children in a state of lethargy. Mary denied having given anything to the children, but was in possession of a cup with dark dregs remaining in it and little Alice said her mother had given her some poison. All three were taken to the home of P.C. Wigington and then to that of Dr McCoubrey where emetics were administered to make them sick.

Alice made a good recovery and by 11 pm was demanding her 'Mammy'. But she refused to believe the pale, unconscious and heavily breathing mite with her was little Charles. The latter died at 3 a.m. and post mortem subsequently revealed laudanum – tincture of opium – still undigested in his stomach.

Earlier Mrs Braithwaite had been taken to Barnsley police station from the doctor's house, where questioning took place while Dr John Blackburn administered further emetics. The unfortunate woman's reply was that she couldn't 'do for herself or children, and didn't know what to do'.

The inquest, held at the Thornley Arms, Dodworth, heard Mr Braithwaite describe his wife as a 'sober woman' and recount how he searched for her, after hearing of the incident at the canal. A letter from his wife was also produced. Part of it read, 'I have borne being as I am until I can bear it no longer. I would take all my children with me if I could as they are not strong, none of them, I think they will come to the same unhappy end as me. I never

thought I should come to such an unhappy end as this but I would rather die than go to the asylum.'

The coroner's jury needed only a short retirement to come back with a verdict of wilful murder, and the following Friday saw the woman before Barnsley Magistrates, when she was described as being 'in a prostrate condition, moaning bitterly and hiding her face with her hands and shawl.'

At the end of July, Dr Blackburn and Wakefield prison medical officer Henry Clarke, informed a Leeds Assize Court hearing that Braithwaite was unfit to plead through insanity. She replied 'Don't know' when asked if she was pleading guilty or not guilty, so the case proceeded as a trial.

Almost all the evidence was given by James Robert Barton, assistant physician at Wadsley Asylum, who said Braithwaite heard voices telling her to destroy herself and saw men coming to stab her during hallucinations. He told how the Lunacy Commissioners had ordered Braithwaite's discharge from the asylum, because old certificates had been used. The new ones required a doctor to read out part of the Act to those being certified. A new certificate should have been delivered to the relieving doctor, but this was overlooked. Mr Justice Grantham had strong words to say about that. He said that a technical alteration to forms, was no pretence that the woman was fit to be discharged or that she might not murder everybody with whom she came into contact.

'The commissioners didn't take the slightest trouble about that; the order was that she be set at liberty. If altering conditions of certificates, they ought to take proper care that the correct forms were conveyed to the appropriate persons, so that people not fit to be at large should at once be placed in confinement again.'

The jury agreed wholeheartedly as they returned a verdict of 'Guilty but of unsound mind'. The other charges of attempted murder and attempted suicide were not proceeded with and the judge said he hoped Braithwaite would get better while ordering her to be detained 'at Her Majesty's pleasure'. As stated, the public outcry was swift and spectacular with the *Yorkshire Post*, the *Sheffield Independent* and the *Sheffield Telegraph* all joining in the attacks on the Lunacy Commissioners. The *Leeds Mercury* probably summed things up best, 'Red Tape has had a lot to answer for in the past, and now wilful murder has been added to the category'.

Less than a week later questions about the tragedy were being asked in Parliament, but the Lunacy Commissioners were never publicly pilloried. They maintained Mary Braithwaite should have been correctly re-certified shortly after her release, but said the doctor who originally certified her declined to do that after a further examination. That claim does not seem to have been either substantiated or refuted. Either way, it was the system that broke down – and little Charles Braithwaite who paid the price.

Victim: ***Edward 'Ned' Batty, clubbed,*** **October 1893**

The discovery of Matthew Fearns' body on the morning of Wednesday August 8th, 1894, set every tongue in Barnsley wagging. The reason was not that the 53 year old gamekeeper met a particularly gruesome end, although he did – suffering blasts from both barrels of a shotgun at point blank range. It was because Fearns himself had been labelled a killer less than a year before.

A young Ward Green miner by the name of Edward 'Ned' Batty, had named Fearns as his killer in a dramatic death bed accusation. His story was supported by his older brother and a coroner's jury later returned a manslaughter verdict against Fearns.

Fearns was employed as gamekeeper to local landowner Mr V. Wentworth subsequently underwent trial at Leeds Assizes. He was acquitted, but his violent death resulted in a flurry of speculation that a murderous act of retribution had taken place. Virtually the entire population of Barnsley, knew that threats had been made against Fearns by members of the Batty family and friends of young Ned; and despite all the evidence pointing to a most unfortunate accident, many were loath to believe that Fearns' death was anything other than a bloody act of vengeance.

We start our examination of this intriguing case with the *Barnsley Chronicle* of November 4th, 1893, which had banner headlines announcing: 'Manslaughter By a Gamekeeper at Worsbrough – A Mysterious Affair'. The accompanying write-up was lengthy and concerned with two separate hearings. The first was the trial of Ned Batty's elder brother Reuben on a charge of trespassing in pursuit of game. The second was the inquest on Ned Batty. Both hearings concerned events that took place on the afternoon of Friday, October 20th, when the Batty brothers were caught on land at the Ward Green side of Worsbrough reservoir. Exactly who owned the land is not clear. It could have been Mr Edmunds of Worsbrough Village, or the Manchester, Sheffield and Lincolnshire Railway Company. Either way, Mr Wentworth, Fearns' employer, held the shooting rights and the brothers had no right to be there.

As Reuben Batty had nine previous convictions for poaching and his brother one, a showdown was only to be expected when Fearns arrived in the company of two 'watchers' by the name of Fred Jagger and John (Jack) Christmas.

Accounts of the confrontation varied from the outset. Fearns and his aides claimed the Battys were among a party of four men, two of whom ran off. They said they found an old rifle, secreted by the brothers, as they approached, and that Ned Batty tried to snatch it back from Fearns. A struggle took place before Fearns, having retrieved the gun, set off with Jagger and Christmas after the two who had run away, leaving the brothers alive and conscious.

The Batty story was that they were on their own and without any firearm. After being prodded and poked by the trio, Fearns removed the barrel from the stock of a gun he was carrying and 'welted' Ned Batty across the forehead with it.

Batty fell into a stony dyke senseless, and Fearns, realising he wasn't faking, said to the others: 'I've finished him – come on.' All three then ran off, ignoring Reuben Batty's entreaties to come back and help him get his brother home.

Reuben half carried and half dragged his brother home, where he was bandaged and put to bed. A doctor was called the following day, after young Ned became delirious. The young miner died of a fractured skull and meningitis the following Tuesday, having recovered his senses for long enough to make his dramatic accusation against Fearns in the presence of a magistrate.

Members of the coroner's jury had three options open to them. If they believed Fearns had deliberately killed Ned Batty, then they should return a murder verdict; if they believed Fearns did strike Batty but in the heat of the moment, then their verdict should be manslaughter. If they believed Batty died as a result of a struggle with Fearns, then their verdict should be one of misadventure.

In the event their verdict was unanimous, manslaughter. That verdict was returned after hearing evidence from Dr J. F. Horne that Batty had the thinnest skull he had come across in 20 years' practice and death could easily have been caused by falling on a sharp stone, or being struck with a gun barrel. The same evidence however, was not sufficient to convince a jury at Leeds Assize Court. Fearns was acquitted and, far from appearing concerned at the threats of violence towards him, later moved to live nearer the Batty home, moving from Dovecliffe, to Worsbrough Village.

So it was that on the afternoon of Tuesday, August 7th, Matthew Fearns picked up his loaded, double barrelled shotgun and left his

home in company with his Airedale terrier, saying: 'I shan't be late'. He was due to meet his assistant George Brown and patrol part of the estate, but he never arrived at the rendezvous. His body was found in a ditch near Barrow Colliery yard at 3 a.m. the following morning by a Hoyland pit deputy called Joshua Smith. His faithful dog was still by his side. Mr Smith chose to inform P.C. Henry King of his gruesome discovery, rather than risk tangling with the dog.

It was easy to determine the time of Matthew Fearns' death – his watch, smashed by the blast, still stood at 6 p.m. while his shotgun, both barrels fired, lay nearby. It also seemed easy to determine how he died. Across the ditch were two wooden sleepers, one of which was rotten and freshly collapsed. His shotgun, both barrels fired, lay nearby. On the other side was a piece of metal which had once formed part of a handrail. There were two marks on that piece of metal which corresponded to the hammers of the shotgun – both of which were broken off the gun. It didn't need a Sherlock Holmes to work out that Fearns had been crossing the ditch, holding the gun by the barrel with its muzzle upwards, when he slipped. The hammers hit the piece of metal and both barrels were discharged simultaneously into the luckless man's body. Ironically, it was Fearns' responsibility to ensure the ditch was safely passable.

Just in case you still think it could have been a skilfully executed murder, I should also point out that summer weather had reduced the dyke to little more than mud, which showed every footprint when steps were taken to recover the body. The jury at the inquest, held in the Edmunds Arms public house, were quick to return a verdict of accidental death. The only puzzle to them was why Fearns' assistant, George Brown, saw neither body or dog, when he crossed the same dyke after Fearns had failed to show up at their planned meeting point.

Looking at the sequence of events in both deaths, must leave us with several questions. If Fearns didn't kill Ned Batty, then who did? And if you discount Reuben Batty as being responsible, then you are left with an unfortunate accident similar to the one later suffered by Fearns. If, on the other hand, Fearns was responsible for Batty's death and not only lied himself but persuaded Jagger and Christmas to lie as well, then you may consider that his death was a form of divine retribution or a quirk of deadly fate.

Incidentally, I should mention that Reuben Batty lost more than a brother as a result of that visit to Worsbrough Reservoir. He was fined 2s 6d and ordered to pay costs by Barnsley Magistrates for trespassing in pursuit of game, despite denying the charge.

Victim: ***Herbert Neatby, head injuries,* April 1894**

A coroner's jury took just five minutes to decide that Barnsley gentleman Herbert Jackson Neatby, committed suicide while temporarily insane. That verdict may have satisfied the people of Leeds, where 26 years-old Mr Neatby met his death, but it never satisfied his father. Samuel Mossforth Neatby, a retired timber merchant who lived in Kensington Road, Barnsley, steadfastly refused to believe his son had taken his own life and made sure the jury knew about it.

After giving his evidence to the hearing, Mr Neatby asked and was given, permission to make a short statement. Part of that statement ran, 'I know of nothing, nothing whatsoever, that would indicate the possibility of suicide, and the letters I have received since the affair occurred lead me to utterly discount such an idea.' He continued, 'Only on Sunday last I saw him and he was as bright and nice as ever in his life.'

Mr Neatby's statement may not have convinced the jury, but it seems as though it was strong enough to raise doubts at the *Barnsley Chronicle*. In its issue of April 21th, 1894, the paper used the headlines: 'Tragic Death of a Barnsley Gentleman – A Mysterious Affair – Accident, Suicide or Foul Play?'

Having sent one of its own reporters to cover the inquest hearing, the paper then went on to give a lengthy and detailed report of the proceedings. To start with, Herbert Jackson Neatby was well known and well liked, having helped in the family business before turning to a career in medicine and undertaking studies at the Leeds Medical School. He was studying for his final examination when he was found groaning in a roadway 27 feet below a bridge in New Station Street, Leeds, at 2 a.m. on the morning of Tuesday, April 17th, 1894.

P.C. Thompson, who found him, arranged for him to be taken to Leeds General Infirmary by ambulance, where it was discovered that not only did he have a fracture to the top of his skull, but also 'considerable bruising' behind his left ear and a number of smaller bruises to his forehead. Mr Neatby died shortly before 5 p.m. the

same day, without regaining consciousness.

Two facts initially led the police to believe that he had been the victim of foul play. The first was that there had been a number of recent robberies and assaults in the roadway known as Swinegate, and up above in New Station Street. The second was the absence of a pocket watch, the universal sign of a gentleman in those days.

But doubts about the 'foul play' theory were raised right from the start when it became clear that the deceased's pockets had not been turned out and some expensive medical equipment, two pocket books and 13d in loose change were recovered from his clothing. Accidental death was also unlikely as the bridge parapet was four feet high and three feet wide.

Medical evidence was also inconclusive. There were no broken limbs to indicate a fall and three separate sets of head bruising were difficult to equate with just a fall. But there was nothing to clearly suggest that Mr Neatby had been the victim of physical assault.

This left the police with the task of finding out about the victim and his movements on the night in question, and that's where they appear to have struck gold.

Mr W. A. Brown, House Surgeon at Leeds Infirmary, told them that Mr Neatby consumed alcohol to excess and also took medicine. In addition he also suffered a form of blood poisoning, and could by his own knowledge of medication, have formed the opinion that the condition was incurable.

Emma Hampshire, a barmaid at the Temperance Hotel, Queens Court, Leeds, told the police and the jury that Mr Neatby had spent the previous Friday night there with a woman and he complained that his watch was missing the following morning. Refreshment house keepers Walter and Alice Pilling said that they, unknown to each other at the time, both loaned small sums of money to Mr Neatby on the Monday; and Alice Pilling said that he had complained of consumption and of spitting blood earlier the same day.

He said there was no 'return ticket', to where he was going.

Mr Neatby, it should be said, left his topcoat, gloves and a medical book with the Pillings to show good faith. Last but not least, Polly Parker of Cross Belgrave Street, Leeds, told the court that the deceased, who was known to her, bought her and another woman tomatoes and sandwiches at 11.30 p.m. on April 16th. While doing so, he told them, 'You can have what you like, for you will never see me any more alive. I am going to commit suicide'. Mr Neatby, who she believed was drunk, then produced small pill box with the word 'Opium' on the lid and advised her to buy the 'Pink', to read of his death the following night.

Coupled together, those accounts would seem good enough to convince more juries of suicide; but large holes did remain.

For example, it was known that Mr Neatby had been out in the company of three other medical students. Why were they not called to give evidence? It was also known that George Dodworth was on duty in a signal box in New Station Street, but he could not remember seeing Mr Neatby there. In fact, there was no evidence that Mr Neatby had ever been up on the bridge.

What happened to the opium pill box? Why didn't Mr Neatby leave a suicide note, rather than speak to relative strangers? That question is even more interesting when you consider Mr Neatby had an invalid brother and sister at home.

What happened between 11.30 p.m. and 2 a.m.? And were those injuries really consistent with a 27 foot fall? Mr Neatby senior wasn't convinced and neither was the Chronicle. As they wrote at the time, 'It has not been conclusively established how he came by the injuries which caused his death and probably never will be'.

I would venture to say that the Chronicle was probably right, and a present day jury would be much more likely to return an open verdict.

Victim: ***Laura Smith, throat slit,*** **September 1894**

Little Laura Smith's murder was bloody and barbaric. At the age of two, the little mite was picked up by her father, placed across his knees and then had a cobbler's knife drawn straight across her throat. The act itself was shocking. So were the similarities between her murder and that of little Charles Braithwaite some three years before. Both counted their age in months rather than years, both were murdered by a parent, and both lived in Cresswell Street, Pogmoor. More importantly, both were murdered by parents who had been admitted to the West Riding Lunatic Asylum at Wadsley Bridge, Sheffield, and later discharged.

The murder of 17-month-old Charles, with laudanum administered by his mother, caused an outcry because Mary Braithwaite was released from the asylum through a 'red tape' technicality.

That was not the case with Laura's father. James Smith was legitimately discharged from the institution, but his 'behavioural problems', had persisted. Of most concern was the fact that, just three days before the gruesome murder, the 36-year-painter and paperhanger had consulted the Barnsley physician, Dr John Blackburn, who unfortunately told Smith there was nothing wrong with him and sent him on his way. Perhaps that was one reason why there was no furore about little Laura's death; it may even go some way to explaining why newspapers of the day didn't even point out the similarities between the two infanticides.

Or perhaps it was the sheer barbarity of the offence which stunted our forefathers' lust for the macabre. While previous murders had often seen the whole town lining the streets to view the passing of funeral processions, little Laura's cortège passed through most of the town without stirring very much attention. True, the Pogmoor public was out in force as four little girls wearing white sashes carried the tiny coffin to the coach, which was provided by the workhouse authorities. But along the rest of the journey to the cemetery interest was minimal.

The reason for this was not lack of publicity. When the *Barnsley Chronicle* announced the murder in their edition of Saturday, September 22th, 1894, reporters were busy preparing a special edition which was on the streets later the same day.

The paper reported that, around 9.30 a.m. on the morning of Friday, September 21, Smith arrived at the home of his next-door neighbour requesting the loan of a cobbler's knife saying that he was repairing the shoes of one of his five children. Neighbour James Gear, complied with the request. The next he knew was the arrival of Smith's eldest son in an upset state.

Ten-year-old John William Smith explained: 'Oh Mr Gear – save me! My father's killed Laura and he's going to kill me.' The boy was followed by Smith, still clutching the bloody knife.

'I've done it,' he said. 'I've killed Laura.'

Smith offered no resistance as Mr Gear took the knife from him and led him into a back yard.

Mrs Gear, accompanied by a Mrs Britton, rushed into Smith's house, where they found Laura lying just outside the bedroom door, her little head overhanging the top step. Mrs Gear snatched up the child, but Laura, her windpipe severed, died seconds later.

The inquest, held on the Saturday at the Tom Treddlehoyle public house, did not take long. The jury didn't even bother to retire before pronouncing their verdict of wilful murder against James Smith. The only witnesses were Mr Gear, Dr Hamilton of Barnsley and young John Smith, who said he was in the bedroom with Laura when his father entered the room, picked up Laura, sat on the bed then used the knife to cut her throat. His mother was out picking potatoes at Wombwell.

James Smith never gave a reason for his actions, either at committal hearings before Barnsley Magistrates or before Mr Justice Collins, who presided at the subsequent Leeds Assize Court hearing in mid December. Smith, who was undefended, did not appear even to appreciate the nature of the charge when it was put to him. He remained silent and a formal plea of 'Not Guilty' was entered on his behalf.

The only additional evidence provided was from his former colleagues at Mitchell Main Colliery, who said Smith was hit on the head by a stone when working there in January. Soon afterwards, he started showing behavioural abnormalities, and on several occasions, had to be taken home from the colliery.

He was admitted to the Wadsley Bridge Asylum, but discharged on May 15th. He soon gave way to 'intemperate habits', although that was put down to depression at being unable to find work.

Evidence was given by the medical superintendent at Wadsley, Dr Kaye and the medical officer at Wakefield gaol, Dr Clarke, who both stated that Smith was not in a condition to know the nature of the crime he had committed. He was suffering from severe mental depression and homicidal mania.

Dr Blackburn, interestingly enough, was not called to give evidence. Confronted with such evidence, all that remained for Mr Justice Collins to do, was to order that Smith be detained during Her Majesty's Pleasure.

The file on the murder of little Laura Smith was closed. It was one death which the public of Barnsley and at least one of its medical practitioners desperately wanted to forget.

Victim: ***Florence Robinson, shot,*** **May 1897**

On Wednesday, May 12th, 1897, Barrow Colliery miner Joseph Robinson walked into the Barnsley shop of Messrs Reynolds and Wadsworth and bought himself a revolver. He then walked to the Shambles Street chemist's shop of Lewis Eastwood and paid 9d for a bottle of laudanum. He had two things on his mind – the murder of his young wife and his own suicide.

Hours later the first part of his mission had been accomplished. 24 year-old Florence Robinson lay in the yard of a house in Mount View, Burton Road, Monk Bretton, with a bullet in her brain. Robinson had to wait until Tuesday, August 17th, to achieve the second part of his mission. In that, he was aided by the noted executioner, Mr Billington and his assistant.

The Robinson story is a sad one – about a couple who couldn't live together, and a man who couldn't live alone.

The story starts on Easter Monday 1889, when Robinson, then aged about 25, married Florence Smith. She was little more than a girl – aged 16 and the daughter of Mr Thomas Smith, a paper maker of 2 Cutty Lane, Old Town. From the outset, their marriage was a story of jealousies, bickering and stress. Originally they lived at Normanton, then moved to the North East for two years, before returning to their home town, to live at Worsbrough Common.

By 1896, they were living in New England, Worsbrough Bridge, and had two children and a 12 week old baby. It was at that time that Florence Smith decided to leave her husband – not for the first time.

The reasons appear to have been twofold. A local girl had had a child to Robinson and gained a warrant against him; and Florence Robinson had laid a charge of aggravated assault against Robinson's brother, then living with them as a lodger. The assault hearing took place in July, when Mrs Robinson not only charged her brother-in-law with assault, but also of threatening her with a revolver. He in turn made accusations about her moral character and alleged that

she had tried to induce him to elope with her.

The magistrates appear to have accepted her version of events by sending her brother-in-law to prison for two months and binding him over to keep the peace.

Living with her mother, Mrs Robinson subsequently took out two summonses for aggravated assault against her husband, both were settled out of court when he agreed to a separation.

But the relationship continued to be stormy, with Robinson persistently entreating his wife to return to him. His actions however, did little to endear him to her. Robinson, then living in the Sheffield Road area of Barnsley, took the baby away from the house, and within weeks the child was dead. He also took another child away and gave it to a stranger, but it was later returned.

On another occasion Robinson 'blackguarded' his wife as she tired to board a horse-drawn bus to attend work as a domestic servant at Birdwell. This attack was seen by his mother who said: 'He was such a blackguard – I couldn't speak to him.'

On yet another occasion Robinson was ordered to pay costs, and bound over to keep the peace to the sum of £10 with ten days' prison in default, after making threats against his wife at his mother's home. Despite this, Mrs Robinson returned to live with her husband three times during the year, though on each occasion she quickly left. The last separation took place nine weeks before the tragic events of May 11th, when Florence Robinson was living at the newly-built house in Burton Road occupied by a Mr Robert Marshall, an engineman at the nearby Monk Bretton Colliery and his invalid wife, who was Mrs Robinson's cousin.

Robinson, it appears, must have waited for Mr Marshall to go to work around 2 p.m. Minutes later he slipped quietly into the house.

The first that neighbours knew of his arrival were his wife's screams of 'murder'. Benjamin Gill and George Clarke ran from their homes on either side of the Marshall house to find the door locked. Looking through the window, Mr Gill saw a shrieking Florence Robinson in a desperate struggle with her revolver clutching husband.

She made a piteous appeal for help to Gill as the contents of the revolver were discharged. Freeing herself from her husband's grasp, she leaped for the door and succeeded in getting it open just before the gun was fired again. She fell forward through the door, her young life spent.

Robinson quickly locked the door again and, by the time Mr Gill had smashed his way in through a window and opened the door to admit Mr Clarke and others, he had consumed the 2 oz. contents of the laudanum bottle. He made no attempt to turn the gun on himself or to stop the gun being removed from him.

Mr Gill tried to give comfort to a hysterical Mrs Marshall, still confined to her bedroom upstairs. He then ran to the nearby Monk Bretton Colliery from where he telegraphed Superintendent Kane at Barnsley police station.

Mr Clarke and others, meanwhile, gave salt and water and mustard and water to Robinson in an attempt to make him sick. Between bouts of vomiting he incoherently spoke of his love for his wife and about how 'neighbours', had told her lies about him.

The inquest, held the following day at the Bridge Inn, Monk Bretton, saw Mrs Robinson's mother, Mrs Jane Smith, tell of her daughter's last meeting with her husband at Barnsley Court House Railway Station the previous weekend. She told of how her daughter again rejected pleas from Robinson to return to him and then boarded the train for Monk Bretton. Robinson turned to her and said: 'Well – she's young, but I will finish her.' He then picked up his little daughter who was staying with her grandmother and kissed her, saying, 'I shall never see thee no more'. In that statement, Robinson was wrong. His daughter, described by the Chronicle as a 'bright-looking lassie aged about four', was present with her grandmother when she gave evidence against him before Barnsley Magistrates on Monday, May 24th.

Charged with feloniously, wilfilly and with malice aforethought killing his wife, Robinson was described as 'listening to the evidence with a calm and quiet demeanour and without showing any feeling', despite the young girl's presence.

The same cannot be said of Mrs Smith, who appeared to be under 'great emotional strain', at seeing him. A packed court house heard Dr Matthew Corrie Halton describe how a bullet was found in the roof of the victim's skull.

They also heard P.C. George Henry Hanson describe how Robinson vomited as a result of the emetics administered and how he was fit enough to be charged on the evening of the murder. His reply to being charged was, 'Yes – I shall never deny it. I hope she's gone to heaven'.

Robinson, who was committed for trial at Leeds Assizes, declined to say anything to the court. He was not legally represented and a charge of attempted suicide against him was not proceeded with. He was equally reluctant to defend himself at the higher court hearing with the result that less than 30 minutes elapsed, between his appearance in the dock and the sentence of death being pronounced. The brevity of the proceedings resulted in the Chronicle's 'Note and Comments' column subsequently announcing it as a record for the latter half of the 19th Century. But as the report continued: 'The case was so clear that the facts stated by the witness did not admit of dispute and the only possible plea that could have been advanced on behalf of the prisoner was that he must have been of unsound mind at the time he committed the deed. Even then the deliberation and method which characterised his assumed madness must have given the lie to the theory.

'We have not heard of any memorial being taken up on Robinson's behalf and it is hardly likely there will be. There were no extenuating circumstances in the case, and Robinson's action at the time of the murder showed that he does not desire life which, in perpetual confinement, would be even worse than death.'

Joseph Robinson was executed by hanging at Armley Jail on Tuesday, August 17th, 1897.

Also executed that day was another Robinson of Thornton, Bradford, who had not only murdered his cousin, but had then locked two people in the house with her mutilated body. That man – Walter Robinson – was described as 'postrate with fear', as the day of execution neared.

Joseph Robinson, by contrast, was described as facing his death with indifference. He ate heartily, slept well, gave no trouble to the warders, gave every attention to the prison chaplain and attended services regularly. In a way, he could be described as a victim himself, a victim of his own blind passion. Be that as it may, the Barnsley public saw him as a callous and calculating murderer and few, if any, mourned his passing.

Victim: ***Mary Ellen Dobson, beaten,*** **November 1897**

No one ever learned why public house pianist Mary Ellen Dobson was beaten up so badly that she died. The only explanation that John Halliday ever gave for his vicious and sustained attack on her, was that she was drunk and broke windows at the house they had moved into only the previous day. But the evidence given by neighbours at the resulting legal hearings indicated that the breaking of windows was the result of the deadly attack inflicted upon her, rather than the cause of it.

That left the people of Barnsley wondering why the 28-year-old Liverpool lassie, with black hair and a 'comely' face, should have suffered the sickening death that she did. All they really knew was that her death was particularly distasteful, even by the standards of Victorian Britain.

On the night of Saturday, November 13th, 1897, she was repeatedly punched and kicked by Halliday. Some of the attack took place inside their home at 4 Back Waltham Street, and some of it outside. At least once, the victim ran from the house in a desperate attempt to escape, but ended up on the ground being punched and kicked by Halliday before he dragged her back into the house. That part of the attack was witnessed by neighbours, but they took little action to intercede on the unfortunate woman's behalf. According to a neighbour's account, one man did want to intervene, but was prevented from doing so by the woman accompanying him.

Those same witnesses also failed to take any subsequent action, despite the fact that they did not see Mrs Dobson again in the days following the attack. As a result, she lay on a grubby mattress in a downstairs living room for almost three days without receiving any medical attention for her injuries.

Perhaps, not surprisingly, she never recovered from her ordeal enough to make a deposition against Halliday, and died twelve days after the attack, on Thursday, November 25.

Until then Halliday had been charged with unlawful wounding; but the death of Mrs Dobson resulted in his being charged with wilful murder, which resulted in the public taking a great deal of interest in the case. Court rooms were always packed whenever Halliday was to appear, partly because of the gruesomeness of the crime, partly because Mrs Dobson was so well known as a pianist, and also because as a pit-sinker, Halliday had worked at many collieries throughout the area.

Before looking at the court proceedings, we should first examine the events leading up to the crime.

Exactly when Mary Dobson left Merseyside for Barnsley is not known, but we do know that she married pit-sinker George 'Cocker' Dobson, at St George's Church, Barnsley, in 1890. At the time of the offence, they had been separated for around 18 months, and the two children from the marriage were living with Mr Dobson at his mother's home in George Street, Wombwell.

Halliday, aged 40, was also a pit-sinker so it is reasonable to assume that she met him through her husband. They lived together as man and paramour for around nine months, before moving into Back Waltham Street, near the Plough Inn, where Mrs Dobson played the piano.

On the night of the offence Halliday had been out drinking with a man named Tom Beresford, who would later be sternly criticised by Barnsley magistrates. The first that officialdom knew of the offence was at 6 p.m. on Tuesday, November 16, when an unnamed person called at Barnsley Police Station and reported the incident.

Detective Sergeant Danby went immediately to Back Waltham Street and was admitted by Halliday. He found Mrs Dobson bearing so many injuries that he failed to recognise her, although it appears she was well known to him. The injuries included a torn upper lip and a torn ear, a wound to the side of the head and numerous bruises and swellings to face, head, hands, wrist and lower parts of the body.

Halliday was arrested and marched to the police station after admitting assault, saying, 'She brought it on herself'.

Dr Ernest Woodhead Blackburn examined the victim before having her admitted to Barnsley's workhouse hospital. Initially she seemed to rally, and on Thursday of that week a group of Barnsley's legal gentlemen, accompanied by the Chief Constable and Halliday, arrived in the hope of gaining a deposition from her.

Unfortunately she was not well enough to make a statement, and the following seven days saw her condition worsen until she died.

On Friday, November 26th, Dr Blackburn informed an inquest,

held at the workhouse, that the cause of death was brain congestion resulting from the head injuries. The inquest also heard a procession of residents from Back Waltham Street, describe events between 11.30 p.m. on the 13th and 1.30 p.m. on the 14th. The accounts differed in many respects but all agreed that Halliday repeatedly kicked and struck Mrs Dobson, while both inside and outside the house.

Annie Thompson, a 17-year-old bobbin turner who lived next door, described how she peered through the broken window of the home and saw Mrs Dobson lying on the bed saying: 'Oh Jack – please don't kill me'. Halliday, who had just lit a pipe, walked across to her and kicked her in the mouth. He then walked to the other side of the room, sat down and continued smoking the pipe.

Ada Holdsworth, aged 14, described how she saw Halliday kick his victim when she was lying on the pavement outside. He dragged her inside after she said: 'Oh Jack don't – I know what you mean. Do you mean to kill me? But aren't you going to do it quietly?'

Some witnesses were reluctant to talk. Next-door neighbour Thomas Hooley a miner, had to be warned by the coroner, of the danger of being accused of perjury or of 'aiding and abetting'. His wife claimed she had offered Mrs Dobson the sanctuary of her home, but the offer had been refused.

Tom Beresford received his criticism after telling the coroner's court how Halliday invited him to drink with him at the old Royal Oak on the Tuesday lunchtime following the attack. He said Halliday wept as he told him that 'Polly' had come home 'beastly drunk' and how there had been a fight and he had almost killed her.

Beresford accompanied Halliday to his home, but despite Mrs Dobson's semi-conscious condition, did not seek medical attention for her. Instead, he arranged for his wife and daughter to visit. Accused of 'lacking manliness' in not informing the police, Beresford said Mrs Dobson would not give her consent to his fetching the doctor. He denied that he had told the defendant that she would be 'all right in a couple of days' if looked after.

The jury retired for 15 minutes before bringing a verdict of manslaughter – rather than murder – against Halliday.

It was therefore on a coroner's warrant and a manslaughter charge that Halliday took his place in the dock in front of Mr Justice Phillimore at Leeds Assizes on December 8th 1897.

Represented by Mr Horace Marshall, at the judge's request, Halliday denied the charge but was found guilty by the jury.

The judge told him: 'It is a terrible crime that you have been

found guilty of.' Then he added, surprisingly: 'Had it not been shown that – by your conduct after the assault – you were sorry and anxious to do what you could for the woman, I should have passed a heavier sentence than I am going to pass. As it is, I cannot do less than to sentence you to twelve years' penal servitude.'

Halliday's reaction to the sentence was not recorded. Nor is it known when, if ever, he left prison to resume his life. Why he became so violent, then, remains a mystery. Was it simply because he took too much drink, or was there a deeper, ulterior motive?

That was the question the judge deliberated as he summed up. He decided that, even if drunkenness was the cause, it could not be used as an excuse to shelter behind.

That, though, was not the only mystery that remained. It is known that when he appeared before Barnsley magistrates, presided over by the Mayor, Alderman Charles Wray, Halliday asked to make a statement about one of the witnesses against him. He was advised to make that statement at the Assize Court but no record exists of its being made.

It is known, however, that Halliday questioned only two witnesses. One was Tom Beresford, the drinking pal, who he tried to suggest had told him that 'Polly' would be all right if looked after. The other was Sarah Hooley, wife of Thomas Hooley. He asked her if she could remember loaning him a pipe on the night of the assault. Mrs Hooley denied his claim, but if it was true, it reflected badly on her. It could also be the case, of course that Mrs Hooley was the woman who prevented the man from intervening in Halliday's attack on his paramour.

One further mystery remains, who did inform the police about the crime? For me, it has to be Tom Beresford's wife or daughter.

The fact that the person responsible was never identified tends to suggest they were afraid of the consequences – and bearing in mind that Beresford was subsequently lambasted for his lack of manliness, they probably had good reason to maintain their anonymity.

Victim: ***Margeret Norman, heart failure,*** **April 1898**

Margaret Norman died in the early hours of Tuesday, April 12th, 1898. The body of the widowed mother of three was found by a neighbour, Mrs Elizabeth Richardson, on the hearth of her home in Wood's Yard, Dodworth Road, Barnsley. One of her children had been downstairs earlier but returned to bed after failing to wake her.

An inquest was held but failed to merit an inclusion in the *Barnsley Chronicle*. The death notice read simply: 'Norman – April 12th at 83 Woods Yards, Dodworth Road, Margaret Norman, widow of John Norman, stone quarry labourer'. It didn't even state her age. That was the sum total of interest shown in the woman's departure from this life – until June 7th. It was on that night that a labourer by the name of Walter Duffy walked up to P.C. Southwick and told him he had murdered Mrs Norman after she had rejected his advances.

Within hours, all Barnsley was talking about Margaret Norman and her death. People were putting forward their own theories about the death based on the facts as they knew them and, as the Chronicle commented, 'The stories lost nothing in the telling'.

By Thursday, June 9th, Barnsley Magistrates' Court was packed with people all eager to see Duffy, as he appeared on the charge of wilfully murdering Margaret Norman. In the event, 'see' was about all they did. As Duffy's name was called, he promptly stepped to the front of the dock – as the Chronicle stated 'apparently not very greatly concerned about the gravity of his position'.

Mr Butler, the Chief Constable, simply asked for a remand to Wakefield jail, saying he wished to contact both the coroner and the Home Office. He added that Duffy had been charged as a result of his own admission, while Duffy himself said nothing save that he had no objection to being remanded. The Chronicle in those days, not bound by the same 'sub judice' legislation which exists today, found the proceedings far from satisfactory. Their article of Saturday, June 11, 1898, headlined: 'Another Barnsley Sensation – Confession of

Murder,' publicly criticised the police for their low-key approach. The criticism read: 'The police authorities are exceedingly reticent about the new direction the case has taken and are refusing to give any particulars as to the precise nature of Duffy's confession.' They followed that by giving a version of the events as they knew them, but whether they gained the sparse details from the police, or from another source is not stated.

Duffy, who lived in Low Thomas Street, Barnsley, the account read, had spent the evening of Monday, April 11th, with Mrs Norman, who had been widowed approximately a year earlier. From 9.30 p.m. to 11 p.m. they were together in the Wire Trellis public house, and afterwards at the Radical Club, before returning together to Mrs Norman's home. Duffy then made 'improper overtures' to Mrs Norman, but she resisted. A struggle ensued in which he strangled her, after which he straightened up the house and went home.

Duffy, according to the report, appeared to have been under the influence of drink when he surrendered himself to P.C. Southwick, having taken part in a wedding festival during the day. However, he seemed sober enough to know what he was doing, and the police attached sufficient importance to his confession to lock him up. Duffy was also alleged to have made similar confessions to other people before turning himself in. Since April 12th, he had regularly dreamed of Mrs Norman and become so wretched that he had no alternative but to confess to the crime and ease his conscience.

About the inquest, the Chronicle said that evidence of Mrs Norman having a weak heart had been produced and the verdict was one of 'death by natural causes, probably through heart disease'. But they added: 'Quite a number of statements are now being made as to evidence which did not come before the jury. As to these, however, nothing can be said until properly investigated.'

Exactly one week later, Duffy was again before the court, this time looking paler and thinner for his week in Wakefield prison, but still quite calm and collected. The courthouse was crowded, many having travelled a considerable distance for the hearing, which again did not last long. Mr Butler addressed the court, saying: 'During the week, I have had communications from the solicitor to the Treasury and the Home Office, to whom I have given every detail of the case and the prisoner's own statement. I have received another communication today asking that he be discharged. In that case, I do not wish to offer any evidence whatever, but ask that he be discharged.'

The statement appeared to take the clerk to the court by surprise. He asked: 'The Home Office do not propose to go on?' – 'No' said Mr Bulter. 'To take it up?' – 'No' he repeated.

Solicitor Mr John Carrington then rose to his feet, saying he had been instructed to appear for the defence but having heard what had been said would make no further remark. The only other words spoken were from the presiding magistrate, the Mayor of Barnsley. Alderman Charles Wray said simply: 'Least said – soonest mended,' before officially discharging Duffy, who was led down the internal steps to the parade room to be released after the crowds had dispersed.

What happened to him after this hearing is a mystery, and leaves us with a puzzle on our hands a century later.

The questions we can ask are numerous. For a start – why all the secrecy? If Duffy's confession was a notoriety-seeking tissue of lies, why was he not publicly pilloried in court or, if the offence then existed, charge with wasting police time. The fact that he wasn't one may think, would seem to indicate his confession was not malicious and he did play some part in Mrs Norman's death.

But if there was some substance to Duffy's confession, then why was the matter not taken further in court?

Legal hearings have occasionally been held to clear a person's name rather than blacken it, conversely they have also been held without much confidence in securing a conviction. The fact that Duffy said he strangled Mrs Norman is interesting in itself. Strangulation would be obvious in the majority of cases, from bruising to the neck, bulging eyes and tongue, with burst blood vessels in the face, but not necessarily so. If Margaret Norman did suffer from a weak or diseased heart, perhaps her death was a combination of a strangulatory attack on her and her heart giving way. That, of course is pure conjecture. With today's development in forensic science, it could be that exhumation of the body, even two months after burial, could quickly establish the cause of death, but such techniques were not available shortly before the turn of the century.

Therefore, all we can say now is that Margaret Norman's death is an intriguing one. It may be that, in the case of Walter Duffy, justice was done. But it must also be true that justice was certainly not seen to be done.

Victim: ***Ann Whitehead, suffocation,*** **April 1899**

By her own son's admission, Ann Whitehead was 'not a sober woman' and her nature was quarrelsome. These characteristics may have made her more liable to come to a violent end, which she certainly did. But that didn't lessen public concern at her being killed on the night of April 1st, 1899.

Perhaps the biggest reason for the concern was the fact that the murder of the 63-year-old widow, was the third to take place in Monk Bretton in a period of 11 years. The township, then administered by its own local authority, was gaining an unenviable reputation for lawlessness. In truth it was not a reputation that Monk Bretton deserved. The first of the three murders had been committed by Dr Burke, who was Irish by birth and the second was by a man called Robinson who had spent most of his life in Barnsley and Worsbrough and only travelled to Monk Bretton, to gun down his wife. But that didn't stop the village, which was renowned for its priory and Quaker burial ground, from having its reputation tainted.

The story of Ann Whitehead is best remembered for the twist in its tail, but we must start at the beginning.

Ann Whitehead had already raised a family with her husband George Whitehead at their home in Market Street, Barnsley, when he died in December 1887. In those days life for widows was not easy and after letting rooms to lodgers and earning some money from millinery, the wiry little woman became a housekeeper. It was in that capacity that Ann Whitehead went to the Littleworth home of William Little, but she stayed there only three months and left early in 1899. But on April 1st Ann Whitehead was back in Monk Bretton. She left her home in Foundry Street, Barnsley, and was soon drinking in the Norman Inn, at Monk Bretton, scene of Dr Burke's murder of his daughter.

She was drinking rum in 2d measures as she told the landlord, Marmaduke Pickles Herbert – better known as 'Duke' – that she was back 'on business'. That business appears to have been trying to get some money from William Little. Miner Alfred Scales later overheard her telling another customer that somebody owed her some money and she would have it. The person to whom those words were addressed was a young glassblower called Richard Thomas Wormald, who had entered the pub separately from her but greeted her as a friend and went to sit with her.

A short time later he said they should go down Littleworth to 'Williams'. Some time later the unlikely couple returned to the Norman Inn but this time Duke decided that Whitehead had had enough to drink and refused to serve her. That was about 8.45 p.m. Shortly after the duo left. Wormald was walking in front in the direction of Rock Crescent or Terrace – now that part of Burton Road between Rotherham Road and the Norman Inn itself. Whitehead who had enquired the time of the next wagonette to Barnsley, was 'staggering' behind him saying she would 'have the landlord's licence for not filling her drink'.

It was then a little after 9 o'clock and that was the last anyone saw of Ann Whitehead alive.

The following morning her body was found by Samuel Cooper, a hydraulic engineman employed at Carlton Main Colliery, at a point near his home in Rock Crescent. Her body was partly under an archway 27 feet below the road.

Ann Whitehead had a broken bone in her neck and had been partially strangled but Dr Stephen McSweeney came to the opinion that the cause of death was actually heart failure due to partial suffocation and shock caused by violence. She had, he added, the liver of a drunkard.

There were no signs of 'violation' to the body, but a pocket had been cut or torn away from her underskirt. It is known that the pocket had contained money earlier on the evening of April 1st. Mrs Hannah Thorneycroft, wife of Thomas Thorneycroft, the landlord of Monk Bretton's Sun Inn, told the inquest that she had served Mrs Whitehead with rum at around 5 p.m. At that time she had two 2 shilling pieces and some coppers in the pocket.

How much that money had been eroded during the evening or whether it had been replenished by the visit to William Little at Littleworth was not known to the jury who sat with the coroner, Mr P. P. Maitland, during the inquest which ran over from Monday, April 3rd into Tuesday, April 4th at the Norman Inn. They had to contend with at least one drunken witness. George Alfred Peaker who lived near Wormald in Littleworth, admitted he had 'had a few glasses'

before giving evidence. After being castigated for early unintelligible answers, he told the court he had been leaving the Norman Inn at 9.40 p.m. on the Saturday night when he met Wormald approaching from the direction of the Sun Inn. Together with one Edward Powell, they went to the Sun where they stayed until nearly closing time and then went home in company.

Not surprisingly, you may think, suspicion had fallen on Wormald even before the opening of the inquest. He had in fact, been arrested less than ten hours after the discovery of the body.

Police Sergeant Grundy told the inquest how Wormald denied all knowledge of the murder, even after his arrest when he said: 'Oh! I don't know nothing about it.' Wormald's story was that he last saw the deceased just after Duke refused to serve her with drink. Then he walked on Cross Street and round the village until meeting up with Peaker and Powell. That story was doubted for two reasons. The first was that Wormald was a local man, but claimed he didn't see anyone he knew while on his walkabout. The second was that

P.C. Hanson said he was on duty near the village cross at the time in question and was bound to have seen Wormald had he passed that way.

Despite this the coroner's jury balked at bringing back a verdict against Wormald. They settled for one of 'Found murdered by person or persons unknown.'

That verdict must have heartened Wormald for his subsequent appearance before the West Riding Magistrates at Barnsley when the *Barnsley Chronicle* commented on his 'jaunty manner with collar up and manifesting no great concern at his serious position'. He must have been even more heartened to hear the prosecutor, Mr J. Carrington open the case by saying the evidence against him was 'purely of circumstantial nature'. Despite that the magistrates did, after a long retirement, decide to commit Wormald for trial at Leeds Assizes and rejected a plea from Wormald's legal representative, Mr Rideal, for bail. But knocking holes in a defendant's alibi was never enough to prove the crime of murder and Wormald was subsequently acquitted. And that might have been the end of the sad story of Ann Whitehead had we not come to the twist in the tail.

On the night of Tuesday, November 28th, 1899, Richard Thomas Wormald left the Hope Inn at Cliffe Bridge at 10.15 p.m. intending to walk home along the canal bank, he never arrived.

However, on the following day his corduroy cap was found floating in the canal. The canal was dragged and re-dragged in the days that followed but nothing was found.

Then – on Tuesday, January 2nd, 1900, a full five weeks after his disappearance, a body was found in the canal between Cliffe Bridge and Littleworth. The grim discovery was made by boatman, George Binns of Field Lane, Stairfoot, who got the body to the canal bank. He was later to explain the non-recovery of the body by dragging saying that section of the Barnsley canal contained 'holes' with nine feet of water in them rather than the six-foot norm.

Despite its time in the water, the body was subsequently identified as that of Richard Wormald. The Chronicle announced the find to Barnsley's public with the headline 'Monk Bretton Mystery – Tragedy follows Tragedy'. It went on to report how the Grand Jury at Leeds Assizes had thrown out the indictment of wilful murder of Ann Whitehead by Wormald 'on the suggestion of the Judge' and how Wormald had returned to Littleworth, with no chance of disproving the charge.

The Chronicle stated that Wormald's position among his friends and companions became, in some senses, a painful one and that 'rumour', had credited him with the intention of either putting an end to his existence or fleeing the country. But that rumour did not appear to be supported at the inquest held before Mr Maitland, again at the Sun Inn, Monk Bretton.

John Beaumont, the uncle with whom Wormald had lived since a boy, said there was 'no trouble' about the court proceedings and Wormald had never seen him 'put out' about the matter at home. He said Wormald was 'too fond of himself and too fond of life' for suicide and, rather than showing signs of depression, he had never been 'jollier' than on the day before his disappearance.

Alfred North Wiseman, the landlord of the Hope Inn, told the hearing that Wormald had accompanied him to buy pigs in Pontefract, on the day of his disappearance. They had returned home for tea before Wormald set off home having 'drank a bit but being quiet sober'. Mr Wiseman added that he had heard the rumour that Wormald was tired of life, but said he had never given any such indication to him.

The only other witness to give evidence before a verdict of 'Found drowned without mark of violence' was returned, was Mrs Ann Peaker of Ann's Terrace, Littleworth, who also said the body showed no signs of violence.

One question which was either never asked or simply not reported was whether Wormald could, in fact, swim. The other question you may ask yourself is whether any marks of violence would be obvious after five weeks in water.

There you have it then. Was Wormald a murderer unable to live with himself? A young man depressed at his name being tainted by a murder he did not commit? The victim of a revenge killing, or a simple accident?

Only Richard Wormald knew the answer.

Victim: ***Mary McGrady, fatal kick,*** **January 1902**

Radcliffe Holden was drunk when on Boxing Day night, 1901, he said he would fight the 'Best man in Barnsley'. Minutes later, the target of his violence was not a muscle-bound man but his frail landlady.

Holden, a 38-year-old miner, kicked Maria McGrady once in the stomach sending her crashing to the floor. He then walked from her house-cum-shop in Boundary Street, Measbro' Dyke, unaware that his single kick had secured her death.

Mrs McGrady, better known as Maria Hinchliffe, had suffered a gallstone condition for eight years, a problem which recurred fairly regularly, despite the fact that she had undergone an operation at Leeds some time before. The result of the kick was that a large gallstone was thrust upwards into her liver and the 59-year-old, twice widowed woman, was to suffer great pain before her eventual death on the morning of January 8th.

By that time, Holden had already been arrested at Gawber and charged with causing Mrs McGrady grievous bodily harm. His response was: 'I know nothing about it. When I take beer it makes me mad.' Still in custody when informed of her death, he stated: 'I knew nothing about it until a week after it happened, I was drunk at the time.'

It is not clear whether Holden, whose Christian name was listed as 'Ratcliff' as well as 'Radcliff' by the *Barnsley Chronicle*, was present at the inquest held before coroner Mr P. P. Maitland at Barnsley Town Hall on Thursday, January 9th, 1902. If he was, he would have heard Mrs McGrady's son, Mr John Hinchliffe, explain that his mother bore Holden no ill will.

When he was called to his mother's home, she had told him she 'felt bad' and that the lodger had kicked her in the stomach when he was drunk. But she added: 'He has always been good to me and, if he returns, I will have him back again.'

Mr Hinchliffe added that his mother had been 'worse than usual' during the last two or three months as a result of her illness but had been able to get about. His wife took over the role of nurse until his mother's death.

The next witness was Emily Ward, wife of Boundary Street miner Henry Ward, who said she was in the habit of calling on Mrs McGrady, shortly before retiring to bed. On Boxing Day night she arrived around midnight to find the house also occupied by Holden, Mrs McGrady's youngest son Charles, and his friend Benjamin Pickering.

Holden was drunk and wanting to fight anyone who came near the door. For some time the party listened to Holden's threats and bad language, which was aimed at 'no-one in particular'. Then Mrs McGrady rose from her seat saying: 'Now that will do, give over because I am getting tired of hearing you.' She then got hold of his collar and told him to sit down and behave himself.

Mrs Ward tried to join in the pacification of Holden by suggesting he took off his boots and went to bed. Unfortunately he turned on her, Mrs Ward became frightened and ceased trying to get Holden to remove what were to become weapons of death, from his feet.

A short time later, Holden seized the boy, Pickering, and told him to fetch his father for a fight. He then made the boast that he would fight the best man in Barnsley. But that was too much for Mrs McGrady, who again got hold of him by his collar and this time pulled him outside through the open door, announcing she would have 'no more of it'.

Holden's reaction was to shout: 'Well done old lass, good old lass' before spending the next 15 minutes marching up and down outside to his own shouts of 'Left, right, left, right'. He then returned to the open door to be confronted by Mrs McGrady saying: 'No Radcliffe, you're not coming in here any more tonight.'

Without a word, he took one step back and kicked her amidriffs. He was already on his way from the house as Mrs McGrady said falteringly: 'Oh dear – he has hurt me with his kicking'.

Mrs Ward's account was corroborated by Charles Edward Hinchliffe, a 'wetter off' at Rylands Glass Bottle Works, who added that Holden was 'always drunk when in money' and 'always noisy'.

Benjamin Pickering, a pony driver, also of Boundary Street, gave an almost identical account, but only after being rounded on by the coroner. Mr Maitland asked him: 'Have you been threatened not to speak the truth?', to which the boy replied: 'My father said that if I appeared at the court he would hit me. But I told him that I would

speak the truth and he said that would be all right.'

The coroner then said: 'I only mentioned it because I knew of it. If you don't speak the truth I will punish you, I will not hit you, but I will punish you.'

The last witness to give evidence was Dr Matthew Carrington Sykes, who confirmed that he had been treating Mrs McGrady for gallstones for four years. Summoned to visit her on January 4th, he found her suffering violent stomach pains, and following his examination he informed the police of the assault. It was also Dr Sykes who carried out the post mortem examination. He said the bruise – about the size of a man's hand – covered a host of internal inflammations and irritations. The worst of those was the wayward gallstone, which he took to have accelerated death and was 'quite likely', to have been caused by a kick.

The actual cause of death was put down to 'septic inflammation of the gall ducts due to irritation of a large gallstone.'

A verdict of death by manslaughter against Holden was returned by the 14-strong jury, but two members dissented from that decision. Nevertheless, the coroner made out a warrant against Holden. He was presented at Barnsley's Borough Police Court on Thursday, January 16th, where he was charged with feloniously causing the death of Mrs McGrady (manslaughter) at 46 Boundary Street, Barnsley.

The only additional evidence to come out at these proceedings was that of Detective Sergeant Evans, who reported Holden's replies, both at his arrest and when informed of his victim's death.

Asked if he wished to add anything, Holden commenced what the *Barnsley Chronicle* described as a 'rambling statement', until interrupted by the Deputy Magistrates' Clerk Mr J. Carrington, who advised that he say nothing, plead not guilty and reserve his defence. That advice was accepted.

So it was that the Barnsley public never heard Holden's version of the events of that fateful night until he took his place before Mr Justice Ridley on Thursday, March 12th, 1902, at Leeds Assize Court. Nor did they learn much about it then.

The Chronicle limited its coverage to one large paragraph, and said simply that Holden asserted that Mrs McGrady was injured by falling rather than by the kick. The jury found the case proved but recommended mercy, and Radcliffe Holden was sentenced to six months' hard labour.

Whether he ever returned to Barnsley is unknown, and we can only hope that in due course he managed to curb his drinking and immature desire assert his manhood. One thing is for certain – Radcliffe Holden may have threatened to beat the best man in Barnsley, but he subsequently proved himself one of the worst, as a result of which Mrs Maria McGrady suffered an agonising and lingering death.

Victim: ***Frederick Winston Shore, 'mercy killing'*, January 1902**

On January 4th, 1902, William Turner jumped into the icy waters of Elsecar reservoir. Clinging to his arm was his friend, Jonathan Dyson, and somewhere near his other arm was a woman and her four-month-old baby. Between them, the two Elsecar men managed to get Emily Shore to the bank, but if they expected thanks, they were to be sadly disappointed. Instead, the 30-year-old Hoyland Common woman said: 'Let me go back in' and tried to escape them. It was only during the subseqent struggle, that the two men spotted the child still floating in the water.

Seconds later, Mr Turner was again in the reservoir, and this time Mr Dyson not only had the problem of holding on to his friend, but also that of preventing Mrs Shore from joining Turner in the water.

The two succeeded in their respective tasks, and little Frederick Winston Shore was retrieved from the water. Unfortunately, however, the rescue gained him only a short reprieve of life – he died three days later in Barnsley's workhouse infirmary. The baby's death was to have two major consequences: firstly, his mother was to be charged with murder, later reduced to manslaughter, and later had to face a harrowing trial; secondly, questions about the running of the workhouse and its infirmary were to be asked at the highest level and staff changes were to result.

The best way of looking at both is probably in chronological order.

Lily Shore was 30 years old when she gave birth to little Frederick. She was the wife of Rockingham Colliery checkweighman Fred Shore and they lived in Sheffield Road, Hoyland Common. Frederick, born prematurely after a seven-month confinement, was never healthy, but his condition worsened during his last six weeks of life. He started losing weight and soon became emaciated. A Dr Norton was called in and his verdict was that the child was unlikely to live.

Lily Shore, it seems, could not come to terms with that fact. She was also further upset by the fact that her father had recently become seriously ill. For six weeks she refused to leave her home and, towards the end of that period, was described by her husband as 'distressed, distraught and strange.'

On January 4th, she awoke to find her husband had already gone to work. It appears she spent the morning drinking, following which she lifted a pair of scissors to her neck and hacked a three-inch wound across her throat. Then, her first attempt at suicide having failed, she took up her baby wrapped in a shawl and walked the two miles to Elsecar reservoir. Amazingly, considering the neck wound, she escaped drawing attention.

So it was that Messrs Turner and Dyson were enjoying a walk round the reservoir when they heard a 'splashing' noise from near the bridge. Mrs Shore never called for help. Her rescuers were unable to elicit any information from her, as they took her first to Skiers Hall Cottage, and later to the Elsecar home of P.C. Eadie. At times she was sullen and at others rambling, they said she appeared exhausted, but at the same time having a wild appearance.

Asked by the constable what she had done 'a thing like that for', Shore replied simply: 'It's drink and other troubles'. She refused to say any more or give her name and address. Dr Ritchie was called in to treat both mother and baby, the latter being described by witnesses as 'frothing at the mouth and cold as ice'. The doctor said that Shore was 'not right' and recommended her being kept in custody.

At 3.30 p.m. – three-and-a-half hours after the attempting drowning, both mother and baby were admitted to Barnsley's workhouse infirmary.

Despite the baby's ordeal, no doctor was called. The only time the workhouse's medical officer, Dr E. B. Collings, saw the child was on his scheduled visit there on the Monday, and even then was not informed the child had been nearly drowned in a reservoir.

He simply prescribed a warm bed and little Frederick Winston Shore duly died at 5 a.m. the following morning.

The inquest was held before coroner Mr P. P. Maitland at Barnsley Town Hall the following afternoon. Among those to give evidence were Mr Shore, rescuer Mr Dyson, P.C. Eadie and Dr Collings, who said the cause of death was 'commencing pneumonia with a prior cause being wasting'.

About the doctor not being informed of the baby's reservoir ordeal, the coroner said: 'It might have been an oversight that he was not told, but it was a very serious one.' After the jury returned a verdict to the effect that death was due to pneumonia accelerated by immersion in water, the coroner said that was tantamount to one of wilful murder and made out a coroner's warrant against Shore.

Dr Collings repeated his assertion that he had not been told the full history of the baby when Shore appeared before Barnsley's West Riding Court on January 24th 1902. The workhouse master, Mr S. J. Crawshaw, later admitted he did not send for a doctor, saying that it was not usual to do so unless requested by a nurse. In this case, the nurse did not think it was necessary.

The remainder of Dr Collings's evidence centred on whether the child had had any chance of survival. His opinion was that the child would have died even if it had not been immersed in cold water and it was also possible that the onset of pneumonia had been caused by something other than the immersion. The defence solicitor immediately applied for the prisoner to be discharged and although he failed in that petition, the magistrates did, subsequently, throw out the capital charge of wilful murder and substituted it with a charge of manslaughter.

Lily Shore took her place in the dock of Leeds Assize Court before Mr Justice Ridley in March the same year, her ordeal was not a long one. She was acquitted on the grounds that her 'strange behaviour at the time pointed to her mind being temporarily unhinged.'

Whether Lily Shore was able to resume her life in Hoyland Common is not known. What IS known is that even before her trial date had been set, publicity was already being given to the working of the workhouse and its infirmary.

While the treatment, or lack of it, given to little Frederick Shore was never directly referred to, it seems likely that it was of some consequence.

The publicity started when the superintendent nurse and another member of staff decided to resign, but rather than simply accepting the resignations the Barnsley Board of Guardians asked to see them.

The Superintendent nurse simply said she had got a better appointment and had 'grown tired' of the workhouse. Her colleague, however, voiced a whole series of allegations against the management there. The matron was summoned to the meeting and the comments were repeated, she said that the allegations were 'quite new' to her.

From the Chronicle's account, we know that some of the allegations concerned the non-arrival of items requested by nursing staff, which the matron explained by saying the items must have gone to the wrong ward. However, the Master, Mr Crawshaw, said such requests were checked while searching for 'useless extravagance'.

That answer prompted the Chronicle to declare: 'In other words it rests with untrained workhouse officials, to decide whether nurses should obtain what they require for their patients.' That article, entitled 'Friction at Workhouse', resulted in allegations and counter-allegations at the workhouse infirmary, and numerous readers' letters, debating how much control administrative staff should have in the running of the infirmary.

For little Frederick Shore, the whole episode came too late. It could well be that his life was doomed from the start and all his mother did was to try to lessen his suffering. If by doing so the inadequacies of Barnsley's workhouse infirmary were shown up, then perhaps his short life was not all in vain.

Barnsley Workhouse – dreaded by the poor and slated by the Chronicle after the death of little Frederick Shore.

Victim: ***William Swann, beaten,*** **June 1903**

Emily Swann did not go to her husband's funeral. As a crowd gathered round her home in George Square, Wombwell, that Wednesday afternoon in June, 1903. For her own safety she was advised that her attendance might not be prudent.

The 42-year-old mother, barely five feet in height, was well advised. The crowd, mainly comprised of women, was hostile as she found out when she opened a window to appeal to them to: 'Let him go quietly'. The reaction of the crowd was such that the window was closed quickly. Emily Swann's last farewell to her 44-year-old husband William, took the form of a farewell wave from that same window. She didn't see the crowds lining the route to Wombwell Cemetery 'seven or eight people deep', as the hearse was preceded by her husband's colleagues from Aldham Glass Bottle Works.

However, she was acutely aware that the large crowd remained outside her home for several hours, with policemen on duty to maintain order. This crowd believed that Mrs Swann, along with her young lover John Gallagher, were guilty of the murder of her husband; and they were right.

Less than seven months later, Emily Swann and John Gallagher paid the supreme penalty at that time demanded by British justice. They were hanged by the neck until dead. As the result of this joint execution, Emily Swann gained the dubious distinction of being the first woman hanged at Armley gaol.

The story of Emily Swann is a sad one. It starts when Gallagher, originally from Middlesbrough, was discharged from the West Yorkshire Regiment for misconduct and arrived in Wombwell where he found work as a labourer at Mitchell Main Colliery. Soon he was lodging at the home of William Swann and his family in George, or Alma Square, just off George Street.

As a glassblower, William Swann worked shifts and soon became suspicious of the lodger and his relationship with his wife. There were several arguments, some of them violent, before John Gallagher, a short but stocky man, sought lodgings elsewhere. However, he did not move far, just across the road in fact to the home of widow Mrs Mary Ann Ward, nor did he stop seeing Mrs Swann, and the arguments with Mr Swann continued.

On May 11th and Thursday, June 4th, 1903, there were blazing rows between the two men ending in violence.

Then, just two days after the June 4th incident, William Swann arrived home at around 6 p.m. to find Gallagher coming down the stairs.

Accounts of what happened vary, only three people knew the truth and William Swann was left in no condition to say anything. It is known, however, that after an angry exchange of words, Gallagher left the house and walked across to his lodgings at Mrs Ward's, where both he and Mrs Swann, had spent most of the afternoon drinking.

Swann then turned his venom on his wife of 21 years. He punched her several times, causing injuries which included a black eye. Some time later, Emily Swann also ran across the road to Mrs Ward's. Where she maintained she intended showing her injuries to Mrs Ward, but many of those present maintained she was more interested in showing them to John Gallagher.

Either way, Gallagher marched straight across to Swann's and shook the door until it opened and there were soon sounds of a violent struggle from within. Perhaps the most impartial account of what took place was given by John William Dunn, who also lived opposite. He said the noise of the fighting was accompanied by cries of from Mrs Swann of 'Give it to the bastard, Johnny, give it to him!'

Gallagher then left the house saying: 'I will murder the swine before morning. If he can't kick a b...... man, he shan't kick a b...... woman.'

Both Mr Dunn and other witness testified at the inquest and subsequent court proceedings, that Gallagher returned to the house a short time later and tried to enter for a third time, but found that he had been locked out by Mrs Swann.

Mrs Swann had a thick bandage over her right eye when she attended the inquest held before Mr Wightman at the Horse Shoe Hotel the following Tuesday afternoon. She said she told Gallagher her injury was nothing to do with him and that he shouldn't go into the house, he did, however and punched her husband to the floor.

She continued: 'I tried to get my husband up, but Gallagher punched me on the chin and knocked me down. When I got up again, Gallagher was hitting him with an armchair.'

As stated, Mrs Swann's version of events was contradicted by a series of witnesses, many of whom had been drinking with her and Gallagher in Mrs Ward's and they described her as 'drunk'.

Many of these witnesses also described how Gallagher danced with joy when informed that Swann had died. More to the point, they noted his comment: 'I haven't bloody well done it', as he laughed and danced.

One fact that weighed heavily against Mrs Swann was the fact that quite some time elapsed, before Dr Foley was called to the scene. Her husband had been dead for some time. He lay where he had fallen in the kitchen, his head was against a cupboard and a poker lay nearby.

Dr George Ernest Atkins, who later performed a post mortem, said death was due to brain haemorrhage, but there were no fractures to the skull. There were however over 20 bruises, four ribs and the breast bone were fractured. Injuries which required great violence with a blunt instrument, such as a poker or boot.

The jury at the inquest retired for only a few minutes, before returning with a verdict of wilful murder against John Gallagher, but added that testimony against Mrs Swann posed the question of whether she was jointly guilty in some shape or form.

Mrs Swann was detained in the Horse Shoe Inn for some time in the vain hope that the crowd of several hundreds outside would disperse. She was 'hooted' by them and had to be protected by police officers. It was in these circumstances that she was advised not to attend the funeral the following day.

Gallagher, meanwhile, had disappeared. After taking Mrs Ward for a farewell drink at the Royal Oak, he had boarded a train for Sheffield, then travelled to Bradford where all trace of him was lost. All the money he had was 10s 6d, obtained by pawning some of his clothes, despite which it was August 4th before he was eventually arrested at his sister's home in Middlesbrough. He was described as 'half-starved' after several weeks on the run.

His arrest was soon followed by that of Emily Swann, and remand hearings before magistrates at the West Riding Court in Barnsley, resulted in huge crowds assembling. Gallagher was described as sporting a 'sickly smile' at one such hearing and Swann a look of 'almost callous indifference'. The evidence was much the same as that heard at the inquest, and the pair were committed for trial on charges of murder, at the West Riding Assizes held at Leeds. Gallagher's defence was that the killing was a crime of passion.

Besotted by love for Mrs Swann and inflamed by passion, excitement and drink, he overdid his role as a natural avenger and protector, but did not intend to commit murder. Mrs Swann's defence was that her actions were 'reprehensible, wicked and sinful' but she intended nothing more than that her husband should receive a 'good thumping.'

The jury retired for half-an-hour before returning with a 'guilty' verdict against them both. It was only then that the jury learned of further damning evidence against Mrs Swann for the first time. It appears that Gallagher, on his arrest told the police that Mrs Swann,

finished off the murderous attack on her husband with the poker. The fact that he made no play on that in evidence may have been chivalry, or because it made little difference as Gallagher was present and made no attempt to stop her.

Assuming the black cap and passing the awesome sentence, Mr Justice Darling told the jury their decision was the correct one, because Gallagher and Swann had continued the attack after their blood had had time to cool.

Gallagher and Swann were executed together at Armley gaol at 9 a.m. on the morning of Tuesday, December 29th, 1903. They met their fate bravely, each having taken comfort from the ministrations of clergymen. As they mounted the scaffold, Emily Swann said: 'Good morning, Johnny'. Momentarily he looked taken aback, but then replied: 'Good morning love'.

Seconds later they underwent a painless and instantaneous death at the hands of hangman John Billington Jnr.

All that remained of them were some heart-rending letters dictated by Mrs Swann to her 80-year-old mother and sisters begging them to love her daughters Eleanor and 'little Elsie' and to give 'little Raymond' a kiss from her.

Accompanying poems were equally touching, but there was one happier note. Emily Swann said she would rather die than be incarcerated in prison. Nonetheless her body remains there, in a grave lined with quicklime.

Victim: ***John Ward, burned,*** **May 1904**

Barrow Colliery trammer John William Ward couldn't stand the names his sister-in-law was calling his mother and sister. 'If you say that again I will come over this wall to you,' he shouted.

Unfortunately Bridget Ward did repeat her aspersions.

John Ward had seconds before been advised not to mix things with his sister-in-law, because the police had been summoned and he would only get himself into trouble. It was advice the 25-year-old should have heeded, but he didn't.

He got up from the doorstep he had been sitting on with friends, and started to climb the wall, saying simply: 'I'm not afraid of her even if my brother is.' Seconds later, John Ward was in agony. As he reached the door of his brother's home, he came face to face with Bridget Ward who was carrying a lighted paraffin lamp. The next his friends knew was that he was a sheet of flame. He reeled back and fell to the floor, and some accounts state that Bridget Ward then emptied the remaining contents of the paraffin lamp over of him.

Be that true or not, by the time the flames were extinguished the Worsbrough Dale man had suffered terrible burns to his face, head, arms, chest and neck and was believed blind in both eyes. He was quickly taken to Barnsley's Beckett Hospital, but staff knew his case was hopeless from the outset, and arrangements were soon being made for magistrates to get a deposition from him the following morning. In the event, Ward lived for eight days despite his face being a 'mass of blisters' and being in intense agony. An inquest heard later that the cause of death, was 'exhaustion from delirium consequent on burns.'

The weeks following his death, on Saturday, May 7th, 1904, were to be busy time for the gossips of Barnsley and in particular Worsbrough Dale. The *Barnsley Chronicle* fanned the public's interest with the headlines: 'Shocking Affair at Worsbrough Dale', 'Lighted Paraffin Lamp Used As A Weapon' and 'Young Married

Woman's Mad Act' published on the same day as the death of John Ward. The editorial described how Bridget Ward had already appeared in court on a charge of inflicting grievous bodily harm on her brother-in-law and she had sobbed bitterly throughout the hearing.

The police evidence at that later hearing was given by Superintendent Quest, who described how Mrs Ward was outside her home in Jarrett's Buildings, Worsbrough Dale, allegedly causing a disturbance by using abusive and offensive language about members of her husband's family.

The victim, who lived with his father over the wall in the next yard, shouted that he would get over the wall to her, but she ran into the house, picked up the paraffin lamp and when he reached the open door of her house, struck him with it. She then upset the lamp over him while at the same time 'using an ugly expression'.

Mrs Ward was arrested the same night, her immediate response being, 'It was his fault – I did it in self-defence'.

But she had then added: 'I am heartily sorry that it happened.'

The first full airing of the facts took place during the inquest, held at Barnsley Town Hall, on Monday, May 9th 1904. Mrs Ward was present and heard her father-in-law, William Ward, describe her as 'violent when in drink' and having threatened to 'swing for her husband'. On a kinder note, he said he had never heard her threaten the deceased, and did not know of any reason she had to be vexed or hostile towards him.

Near-neighbour Clara Swift told the hearing how Bridget Ward had been served with a summons for causing a public commotion on another occasion earlier on the night of the death of John Ward.

Mrs Ward was excited and upset and shouted that she would 'swing for the Irish cowards', before going off down the road muttering to herself. An hour later, she was back at home arguing with her husband, until he left to fetch a policeman to quieten her down. She continued to shout from the doorway that she would 'make him pay'.

It was Mrs Swift who gave the damning evidence against Bridget Ward, that she had poured the remainder of the lamp's paraffin over the victim, after he had reeled backwards out of the doorway.

Clara Swift claimed that Mrs Ward uttered the words 'You have got it, you...', at the same time as she poured the remaining parafin onto the already burning victim of her attack. Fortunately for Mrs Ward other witnesses were unable to verify this.

Collier Abraham Robinson, of Cowards Court, Worsbrough Dale,

also suggested that the verbal abuse between the in-laws was not all one-way traffic. John Ward, he claimed said to his sister-in-law: 'Shut up, you Irish pig, and go into the house, we've had enough of your trouble.'

Mr Robinson said he did not see Mrs Ward pour paraffin over John Ward, but did say she appeared to strike him with the lamp.

The coroner's summing-up was simple: 'If they believed John Ward was struck in the heat of temper, the jury should return a verdict of manslaughter. If they believed there was deliberate intent, to kill, then the verdict should be murder. The jury opted for the manslaughter verdict. When Mrs Ward reappeared before Barnsley magistrates on May 16th, she was charged with manslaughter. The court was crowded, but she was much more composed and, said the Chronicle, 'Put several intelligent questions'.

She also subpoenaed two witnesses to appear on her behalf, but it is doubtful whether they helped her case.

One was Emily Cauldwell, also of Jarrett's Buildings, who said she thought both parties had struck at each other, but Superintendant Quest then revealed she had earlier told Sergeant Grundy that she only saw Bridget Ward hit her brother-in-law, John Ward, with the lamp.

Mrs Ward's second witness, Grace McDonald, again of Jarrett's Buildings, admitted under cross-examination that she saw Mrs Ward raise the lamp and hit John Ward on the forehead with it.

The hearing closed with Mrs Ward being remanded in custody to stand trial at Leeds Assizes. She did however successful apply to see her father and children, and for legal representation under the new 'Poor Prisoners Defence Act'. She was assigned lawyer Mr Rideal.

The first the public heard of Bridget Ward's defence, was at the Assize Court hearing, held at Leeds in early August. The 32-year-old mother said simply that she picked up the lamp to look for her missing door key. At that moment, John Ward had rushed in and struck her. The lamp fell to the floor. She did not strike him with the lamp, nor did she pour oil over him while he was down. She said that she and John Ward were on the best of terms and that she was 'sorry from the bottom of her heart for what had occurred.'

The jury believed her.

Thirty-two-year-old Bridget Ward was discharged when they found there was insufficient evidence to convict her of manslaughter, and tearfully she addressed Judge Channell, 'Thank you My Lord. Long life to you'.

As Bridget Ward walked out of that court, she also walked out of the Chronicle columns which her name had occupied for over three months. Whether she returned to Barnsley, her native Ireland or elsewhere is not known. We can only hope she made a new home for herself and her children. Whether she deserved that opportunity is another question.

Similarly, we know very little about her earlier history, apart from her being of Irish extraction and having a stormy marriage. One witness before Barnsley Magistrates, Sarah Cope, did claim Mrs Ward was drunk on that fateful night of April 29th.

Mrs Ward, who was weeping, denied that by saying she had drunk two glasses only, adding to that her husband had given her 4d, because she had been 'badly.'

We have to rely on Mr Robinson, again, for a description of John Ward. That description was of a 'sober, quiet and steady young fellow.' I think we can also presume he was not vindictive by nature, for all he said in his deposition to Mr Fred Waters, assistant to magistrates clerk Mr J. Carrington, was that Mrs Ward 'either threw or struck him with the lamp'. Hardly damning evidence against someone who had condemned him to an agonisingly painful death from third and even fourth degree burns.

FOOTNOTE — For those interested in old buildings, Jarretts Buildings were situated at the bottom of High Street, Worsbrough Dale, near the Masons' Arms. Built in 1858, they were condemned as insanitary in 1957 and demolished the following year. It was only upon demolition that it was discovered that they had been built right up against a much earlier building, at that time a butcher's shop, completely obscuring a fine stone mullion window and doorway.

That shop was originally the 'Buttie' shop, for the Darley Main Colliery. Colliery employees were given brass tickets as part of their pay which they could exchange at the shop for goods. But the practice of making shop profits from wages was frowned upon, hence the 'Truck Act' of 1831 which was intended to stop employees being paid in goods rather than cash.

The shop's mullion windows and doorway are now open to view and in service. Jarretts Buildings features again in a later 'Black Barnsley' profile.

Victim: ***Trubshaws, mother and sons beaten,*** **November 1904**

Beatrice Trubshaw's last words were: 'Ethel – save the children'. Unfortunately, that impassioned plea failed. Not only did the 30-year-old daughter of one of Barnsley's most prominent businessmen lose her life, but so did both her children.

Four-year-old Gordon Hamilton Trubshaw, echoed his mother's words with the pleas: 'Oh Daddy don't kill me,' but even his innocent appeal was ignored; and his 10-month-old brother, Walter Kenneth Trubshaw, fared no better. Both died in an orgy of violence at the hands of their crazed father, Walter Henry Trubshaw. They were repeatedly struck about the head with a policeman's truncheon and a heavy ash staff before falling unconscious. Their father then tried to somehow atone for his action, by slashing his own throat with a razor.

Although the gruesome tragedy took place in Mexborough, in the early hours of November 15th, 1904, the events shocked the public of Barnsley to the core. They knew Mrs Trubshaw as the daughter of Mr J. W. Dobson, of Kensington Villas, Huddersfield Road, Barnsley, a businessman and churchwarden at Barnsley Parish Church and a member of both Barnsley Town Council and the West Riding County Council.

Mr Dobson had raised a large family and all had done well. His sons had followed him into the glass industry, and his two eldest daughters had married Mr Crowther Sugden and Mr A. McLintock, both prominently connected with Barnsley trading houses.

Beatrice Trubshaw, his third daughter, had settled for marriage to a man employed by her father in the commercial department of his glassworks firm. But Walter Henry Trubshaw, the son of a Warwickshire workhouse master, had been tipped to go far. He was a pleasant young man, well respected by all who knew him, and was also identified with the local detachment of the Queen's Own Yorkshire Dragoons, holding the rank of sergeant as well as being the secretary of the Corps. His splendid physique had enabled him to excel at indoor athletics and he often filled in as corps instructor. He was also an expert swordsman, having won the Regimental Fencing Trophy, the Silver Sword.

The couple had been married by Canon Kirby at Barnsley six years before and Mr Trubshaw had continued to work for his father-in-law. But when, four-and-a-half years later, the company suffered financial problems , Mr Trubshaw secured a similar position with the New Don Glassworks at Mexborough, operated by Messrs Peter Waddington and Sons.

Mr Dobson's firm continued to trade in Barnsley as Messrs Dobson and Nall Ltd., but he had transferred his financial interests to another glass concern.

His son-in-law remained at Mexborough, where he purchased Scarrington Villa, in the respectable residential area of Adwick Road, and was soon filling the role of sidesman at the local church. From the outside, they seemed a quiet and respectable couple, bringing up their two sons as good God-fearing people, and so they were until November 1904.

On Sunday, November 13th, Mr Trubshaw was again sidesman at the church, but the following morning he complained of being ill. He did not go to work and didn't rise from his bed until 5.30 p.m. At around 9 p.m. their home was visited by next-door neighbours, a Mrs Ellis, and a Mrs Beatrice Waller, who found Mr Trubshaw 'trembling' visibly, as if he had a cold, and sent they back home for some sweet nitre.

At 10.30 p.m. Mr Trubshaw retired to the front bedroom already occupied by his two sons. Mrs Trubshaw followed him to the same room a short time later and the only other occupant of the house, 15-year-old servant girl Ethel Hill, went to bed in a nearby room.

For what happens next, we have to rely on the servant girl's account. She said she was awakened around 3 a.m. by her mistress shouting, 'Oh Ethel – save me!'

She opened the door to the landing to see Mrs Trubshaw in a desperate struggle with her husband, he had a truncheon in his hand and was striking her with it. It was at that time that Mrs Trubshaw had made her desperate plea for the girl to rescue her children. The girl ran forward as if to intervene but when Mr Trubshaw made menacing gestures towards her, she ran back to the safety of her own room. As was hurriedly dressing, she heard a series of loud 'thuds' and screams from the adjoining room. Above the din she heard Mr Trubshaw shouting: 'Die Beatrice, die love!' and an emotional 'Don't Daddy', from young Gordon.

Ethel Hill was shaking uncontrollably and unable to speak through fear when she arrived at the back door of the home of Mrs Ellis and her clothier husband, Lowther Ellis. She didn't need to speak, they had already been awakened by the screams and had dressed hurriedly.

With Mrs Ellis holding a candle, the couple proceeded next door. Then, however, Mrs Ellis's courage failed, and it was left to Mr Ellis to bravely enter the blood-spattered bedroom.

Mrs Trubshaw lay insensible on the floor, the baby on the bed and

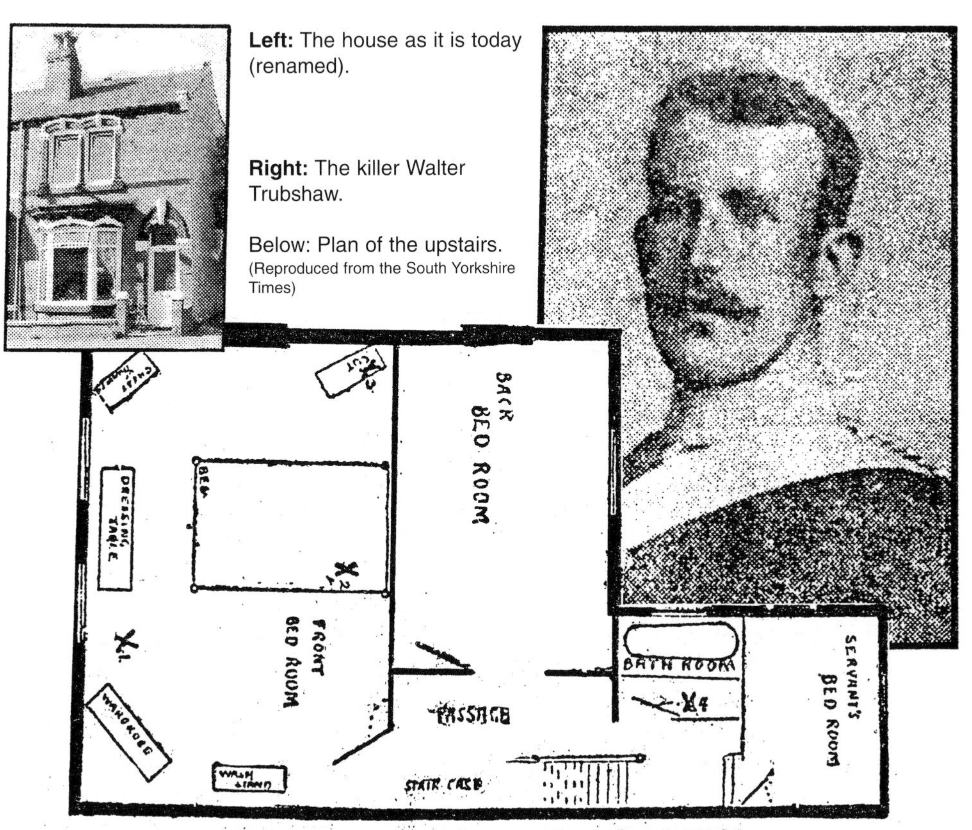

Left: The house as it is today (renamed).

Right: The killer Walter Trubshaw.

Below: Plan of the upstairs. (Reproduced from the South Yorkshire Times)

THE SCENE OF THE TRAGEDY.

PLAN OF THE BEDROOM FLOOR OF SCARRINGTON VILLA. Key:—

—The spot where Mrs. Trubshaw's body was found.
—Where the body of the younger child, Walter Kenneth, lay.
—The cot containing the body of Gordon Hamilton, the elder child.
—Where the body of the murderer and suicide was found.

young Gordon in the cot. Of Mr Trubshaw there was no sign. It was not until after the arrival of Inspector Watson, Sergeant Matthews, P.C. Wood and doctor partners Gardener and Hatherley on their bicycles, that the body of Mr Trubshaw was found slumped behind the bathroom door. He had a large wound on the left side of the neck and an open razor lay nearby.

Mrs Trubshaw and both her sons were still alive amid the broken ornaments and wash jug of the bedroom, but the doctors were unable to be of any assistance. Mrs Trubshaw died without gaining consciousness and was closely followed by her two loved ones. All had suffered skull fractures.

The inquest was held at the Mexborough Montagu Cottage Hospital with the district coroner, Mr D. Wightman, opening the proceedings by saying he had never had to inquire into such fearsome events. The first witness was Mr Crowther Sugden, of Huddersfield Road, Barnsley, who said he could not account for the tragedy, he knew of no financial problems, no recent depression or history of insanity.

Ethel Hill was weeping even before being called to give evidence. She said she had been the family's sole servant for the last five months and had never seen the slightest quarrel between Mr and Mrs Trubshaw during that time. She added, however, that Mr Trubshaw had been complaining with increasing regularity of headaches and had been treated by Dr Gardener for whooping cough.

In his evidence, Dr Gardener said a 'cough' had worried both Mr and Mrs Trubshaw, the former fearing that it was consumption (tuberculosis). He said he had assured Mr Trubshaw he could find no evidence of the disease, but added that Mr Trubshaw 'could scarce believe it was not so'. Dr Gardener concluded by describing the couple as 'passionately fond' of the two boys, but the youngest had suffered a series of ailments which had broken their parents' rest at night.

In his summing-up, Mr Wightman referred to Ethel Hill's evidence that Mr Trubshaw had suffered severe pains in his head, and said it was rather unusual for a man of 30 to stay in bed until 5.30 p.m. merely for a headache. He told the jury the only question they had to consider was the state of Mr Trubshaw's mind at the time of the tragedy.

The jury returned a verdict that Mr Trubshaw killed his wife and two children and then committed suicide during 'temporary insanity', and expressed their sympathy to relatives. The foreman added that Mr Trubshaw had been held in 'very high esteem' by all the townspeople of Mexborough.

The *Barnsley Chronicle* echoed those sentiments on behalf of the people of Barnsley, describing Mr Trubshaw as a 'genial fellow, much respected and renowned for his straight-forwardness and kindly disposition, which meant he quickly made friends.' The article added, 'That an admittedly affectionate husband and father should exterminate all near and dear to him and then do away with himself leaves no reason to doubt that a sudden attack of maniacal frenzy was responsible for the awful catastrophe'.

The Chronicle added one more fact – that Ethel Hill was 'provident' in surviving that night! Although she closed the door of her room before fleeing the house, the police discovered that the room had been entered and items strewn about, presumably by Mr Trubshaw in a search for her.

It seems therefore that Mr Trubshaw had intended to kill once more before taking his own life and had young Ethel Hill been brave enough to respond to her mistress's last request, she would almost certainly have suffered a similar fate.

Victim: ***Arthur Pyrah, disappeared, April 1907,*** **1664**

Arthur Pyrah may have been a victim of murder... or he may not. Equally the 22-year-old Higham man may have been the victim of a tragic accident, or he may have lived to a ripe old age many miles away from Barnsley. The truth is that we simply do not know what happened to the short young miner... and neither did our grandparents.

Conjecture was rife at the time of his disappearance back in 1907. His family seemed to take the view he suffered an accident while working at West Silkstone Colliery while his friends believed that he may have been killed and his body concealed. The colliery management and the authorities appear to have opted for a third hypothesis: that the bachelor decided to disappear suddenly and make a new life for himself somewhere else.

The mysterious disappearance of Arthur Pyrah is a story which began on Monday, April 21st, 1907, when shortly after lunch he left his parents home at 8 New Hill Road, Higham, to walk to West Silkstone Colliery, close to Silkstone railway station.

He was not absolutely familiar with that colliery, but he was used to underground working, having previously worked at the nearby Church Lane Colliery, until it was damaged by fire. At around 2 p.m. he went down the pit with about 30 others. He had with him two pit lamps and his check, which he hung on the board at the pit bottom.

No-one can say for certain that they ever saw Arthur Pyrah after that. At 10 p.m. that night, his colleagues returned to the surface, and so did both Pyrah's pit lamps, but his check remained on the peg board at the pit bottom. According to colliery management, the check was spotted and deputies searched the pit, but nothing was found.

Arthur Pyrah never returned home and his coat remained unclaimed on the pit top.

Some time later, all the men who worked with Pyrah on that

afternoon shift were questioned about him. None could give any helpful information about his movements underground, and all emphatically denied taking his lamps to the surface. The questioning did little to allay the fears of his relatives, who were convinced that he had been lost in the workings.

A second, thorough search of the pit was carried out, but no trace of Pyrah could be found. The pit was also explored by Mr J. R. Robinson Wilson, His Majesty's Assistant Inspector of Mines, who afterwards said he was 'well satisfied' that Arthur Pyrah was not in the pit, adding that his view was shared by every individual employed by the firm.

The latter assertion, however, does not appear to have been quite true, as friends and relatives of Pyrah were far from convinced.

Some put forward the theory that Pyrah had drowned in the pit, others that he had fallen through to older, disused workings, but both were discounted by the colliery manager, who pointed out that the only water in the pit was in the sump and that was only a foot deep. Also, it was highly unlikely that any access to old workings could open and close again in a short space of time, leaving no trace.

The manager stated he was quite satisfied that Pyrah had left the pit during the Monday evening, he could have got out unnoticed in the normal course of drawing off coal. His view appears to have been enough to allay the suspicions of the *Barnsley Chronicle* editorial staff of the day which, oddly enough, did not print his name.

Their report, printed on Saturday May 4th and headlined 'Higham Man's Mysterious Disappearance – Last Seen In Pit', did however, quote the manager as saying that Pyrah might have been seen after leaving the pit. One unnamed employee had seen someone 'similar in appearance to Pyrah', on the pit bank at the end of the shift. He was said to have spoken to the man and received the reply that he was 'waiting for his pals'.

With the benefit of hindsight, such assertions hardly seem adequate to account for the disappearance of a human being.

Had one been held, an inquest, would have required people to give their name and to have sated exactly what they saw. The problem was that the prerequisite for conveneing an inquest in those days, was a dead body. In Arthur Pyrah's case, there was no body, though many would say that a coal mine can be as good a place as any to conceal a murder victim.

That doesn't mean to say of course, that Arthur Pyrah's body now remains entombed somewhere under Silkstone. It could well be that he left the colliery unnoticed and set off in search of a new life.

But if that was the case, why should he do it so dramatically, causing so much grief and uncertainty to family and friends? One thing is certain: if he had determined to write his name into local history books by setting an unanswereable riddle, then he certainly succeeded. Each week, month and year that passed increased our forefathers' speculation rather than diminishing it; and in many cases, that speculation was passed down from one generation to another.

At the time of writing, Mr Willie Frith, who lived in retirement at 72 Abbots Road, Lundwood, still recalled his grandfather talking to him about the strange disappearance of Arthur Pyrah. His grandfather was Amos Newton who, during the First World War, was checkweighman at Barnsley Main:

'My grandfather lived at Silkstone around the time of the disappearance and presumably often talked to the colliers there. He told me that miners at the pit really became suspicious a short while after Pyrah's disappearance when two Irish miners left the pit, and departed the area. Their departure made many miners suspicious that they had killed Pyrah, thrown his body into the 'gob' and then drawn it off. They subsequently returned his lamps to the pit top to make it look as if he had left, but they forgot about the check.'

Mr Frith added that, while that theory gained credence with every passing day, there was still no proof, and the possibility of trying to re-open likely sites was not only financially offsetting but possibly dangerous.

The disappearance of Arthur Pyrah therefore seems to be a mystery that will remain unsolved.

Old West Silkstone Colliery

Victim: ***Thomas Tingle, stabbed,*** **January 1911**

Thomas Tingle was very popular with fellow members of West Melton Working Men's Club. On Sunday, January 29th, 1911, he topped the poll in a club ballot for new committee members... The following night he was murdered there. The 28-year-old miner crashed to the floor from his chair, his life-blood gushing from a stab wound in his neck and he was dead within minutes. Thomas Tingle died because he could not resist another man's invitation to knock his cap off, he had no idea that Willie Samuel Felton had murder on his mind when he made the invitation.

The murder of Tingle was a crime that shook the population of West Melton and the surrounding area. Over 2,000 people are estimated to have waited outside the subsequent inquest hearing. They were not after Felton's blood, more in a state of shock that such a trivial incident could have led to the death of such a popular young man.

Felton and Tingle were known to each other before those fateful events of January 30th, but there was no history of any bad blood between them. Felton, a 33-year-old father of four, had arrived in West Melton from Oldham, Lancashire, some four or five years previously. He subsequently gained employment at Wath Main Colliery where Tingle also worked. By the time of the crime Felton had undertaken several different jobs before becoming a carting contractor.

Felton, who lived at Albert Road, West Melton, was in West Melton Club that night as early as 8.45 p.m. and was not a very happy man. A reply of 'rotten', preceded by a swear word, was given in answer when someone asked him how he was getting on and he continued, 'Everybody has turned against me at this club and the other one'.

Later, he said: 'I have only while Friday and I'll do somebody in and that man is in this room.' His words were accompanied by another oath. A short while later, he commenced playing cards with three other men in the club's games room. The session lasted until around 10.45 p.m. when Felton got up and went to the door. Sitting at a table in the main room was a committee member by the name of John Williams. Felton addressed him, saying, 'I see you have got on the committee again all right?'.

Williams's answer of 'Yes', produced another vulgar remark from Felton, whereupon Williams told him he would be thrown out of the club unless he behaved himself. An exchange of strong words followed, and it was at this point that Thomas Tingle arrived on the scene. Witnesses described how he was laughing, in a joking manner, as he took hold of Felton's cap and threw it to the floor.

Felton retrieved the cap saying, 'There's another committee man', his words punctuated by further swearing... 'The committee men seem to be picking at me.'

Felton then announced that he was going out and that they could knock his cap off again when he came back – if they liked. Three or four minutes later, Felton re-entered the room and sat down at Tingle's table. He said: 'Tha knocked my cap off before I went out – knock it off again.'

Unwisely, Tingle accepted the challenge. Almost simultaneously Felton's hand went to his waistcoat pocket and produced an open-bladed pocket knife. Tingle was already bleeding to death before those around him realised what had happened.

Immediately Williams collared Felton. The knife dropped from his blood-drenched hand on to the table as Felton turned to him and said, 'I can do the same for you'. Despite that, the two men sat together as some men tried desperately to render first aid to Tingle and others ran to summon the police and a doctor.

Before their arrival Felton remarked coolly, 'What I have done I have done in my sober senses, and that man that is laid there has got what he asked for'. Felton was still largely unrepentant when charged with causing wilful murder the following morning. He said: 'I was pecked at – he took my cap off my head and turned it inside out and threw it on the floor. I don't know how it happened. I have got depressed these last few weeks that I have not cared what came. Everything I have touched has gone wrong and I am tired of it, but this will end it all.'

Felton was present at the inquest, held before Deputy Coroner Mr Kenyon Parker, on Wednesday, February 1st. The hearing opened with Dr George Hall Johnston saying the cause of death was loss of blood from a neck wound five-eighths of an inch long. The thrust had cut through the ear lobe and into the neck – piercing the jugular vein.

A series of witnesses then gave their versions of the events leading to the death of Thomas Tingle. All seemed to agree that Felton was under the influence of drink but was not drunk. In his summing-up, the Deputy Coroner told the jurors not to run away with the impression that a verdict of wilful murder would mean the prisoner was 'done for' and that he was convicted straight away, he would receive a fair trial. Twelve of the 13 jurors then agreed on a verdict of wilful murder.

Felton showed no sign of anxiety or emotion, as he was committed for trial on a coroner's warrant. He was hurriedly taken by cab through the crowds outside.

It was on Tuesday, March 21st, 1911, that Felton appeared before Mr Justice Horridge at Leeds Assizes, on a charge of wilfully murdering Thomas Tingle, of Winterwell Road, West Melton.

Among those giving evidence was committee man John Williams of Victoria Road, West Melton; and Joseph William Longley, of Winterwell Road, who caused some amusement as he described Felton's games of cards and gave Felton's description of beer as 'lunatic broth'.

Felton, he added, was normally a peaceful man who had been teetotal for some months prior to January, and was thought to have recommenced drinking because of depression about poor trade.

Although Felton denied the offence, he did not call any witnesses on his behalf, while his defence rested on his counsel's statement to the jury. Mr S. Fleming appearing for Felton, told them that the evidence given to the court, could not reasonably lead them to the conclusion that Felton intended to commit murder. In fact, rather the opposite was the case. The evidence indicated that Felton's 'whole demeanor showed that his brain was not in normal or healthy condition.'

Following a 35-minute retirement the jury's verdict of 'guilty' was accompanied by a strong recommendation to mercy. Felton, knowing full well he was facing the death penalty, hesitated when he was asked if he had anything to say. Then he said simply: 'I am not guilty.' The judge told the jury he agreed entirely with their decision before turning to Felton and saying:

'Your wicked way of giving in to drink and passion caused you to kill a fellow creature. The law has only one sentence for that – it is not my sentence – it is the sentence of the law.'

Felton lived under the shadow of the death sentence for a fortnight, until a reprieve came in the form of a letter from the Secretary of State at the Home Office. Signed by 'obedient servant'

E. Blackwell and addressed to Felton's solicitor, Mr W. M. Gichard, the letter stated, 'I am directed to acquaint you that the Secretary of State has felt it appropriate under all the circumstances, in advising His Majesty to respite the capital sentence with a view to penal servitude for life'.

The *Barnsley Chronicle* closed its coverage of one of the area's bloodiest murders by saying a 600-signature petition had been raised in the West Melton district asking the Crown for clemency, and an even larger petition raised in Felton's home town of Oldham.

While Thomas Tingle was obviously a popular fellow in West Melton, it seems Willie Samuel Felton was not altogether friendless, despite his clearly premeditated knife attack.

Only he really knew whether that attack was intended to kill. We can only wonder what he meant when he said: 'I have only while Friday and I'll do somebody in, and that man is in this room.'

According to Mrs Tingle's evidence to the inquest, Thomas Tingle was still at home when those words were uttered. In the light of this we could reasonably conclude that Tingle was not the intended victim, and that the original target of Felton's deep-seated venom was John Williams or, possibly some other committee member. That person, whoever it was, escaped an appointment with death when Tingle re-focused Felton's attention onto himself by knocking off the killer's cap.

Victim: ***William Hammond, stabbed,*** **November 1911**

At around 7.30 p.m. on Friday, December 15th, 1911, a postman walked to the door of 10 Jarratt's Buildings, Worsbrough Dale, to deliver a letter. The letter was intended for a frail bespectacled old lady, by the name of Charlotte Hammond and it was probably the most important communication the postman ever carried. It was certainly the most important Charlotte Hammond had ever received.

The letter had been posted in London. It told her that the then Home Secretary, a Mr McKenna, had 'felt warranted' in advising His Majesty the King to respite the capital sentence hanging over her 39-year-old son.

It was a letter all the Barnsley area had been waiting for. William or 'Billy' Hammond had been scheduled to hang on Tuesday, December 19 at 9 a.m. for the wilful murder of his 73-year-old father, also called William. The killing was bloody and brutal and there was no doubt that Billy Hammond was responsible. There was however considerable doubt, as to whether he was completely responsible for his actions, and that had prompted over 3,000 people to sign a petition for clemency.

The interest in the case was immense. A *Barnsley Chronicle* reporter was soon at the home of Mrs Hammond and a special edition announced the family's elation.

As the billboards went up at the Chronicle's office in Peel Square to announce the paper's exclusive, large crowds soon gathered to shout their own delight.

Those early purchasers were soon out and about telling others how Mrs Hammond knew the postman had been to her house because her dog had barked. She ran downstairs, picked the letter up and tore it open, but was unable to read the good news because of her failing eyesight and great excitement. Her grand-daughter later obliged.

As soon as possible, Mrs Hammond was on her way to Wakefield prison where she found her son had already been transferred from the condemned cell. As she flew to his arms, she exclaimed:

'God bless King George, his good Queen, and mother, and the Home Secretary for listening to a poor woman's prayer.'

Her son's tearful reply was, 'Aye, mother – God bless 'em'.

Later the same day, Mrs Hammond sat down and wrote a letter to the Chronicle, thanking the paper for its help in supporting the reprieve petition and everyone else who helped towards that end.

The granting of the reprieve meant of course, that Billy Hammond faced a sentence of penal servitude for life, but the vast majority of Barnsley inhabitants preferred that to the death sentence. The biggest single reason for the reprieve was the fact that Billy Hammond had been the victim of a roof fall at Barrow Colliery a year before he murdered his hapless father, since when he had complained of head pains, failing eyesight and insomnia. Many people were on record as saying they had detected a change in Hammond's disposition and that gave the public grave doubts as to whether he should pay the supreme penalty for his crime.

Our story begins at 10 p.m. on the evening of Saturday, November 11th, 1911, when Billy Hammond arrived home at Jarratt's Buildings, after spending the evening drinking in Barnsley.

At home were his father, mother and their grand-daughter, Mrs Priscilla Fallas.

The father, who had lost a hand early in his life, greeted his son's return with what the Chronicle could only term a 'disgusting comment' and the words: 'Hey, tha's come home brussen again, tha pig.' Billy Hammond's response was almost immediate. He walked over to the kitchen dresser, took from it an ordinary dinner knife and announced:

'Father, tha must say no more or I'll mak' yo' know.'

Unfortunately for him, it seems the old man did then mutter something else and Hammond advanced menacingly.

His mother tried to intervene saying: 'Billy don't – I'll go and fetch Tom Bramham'. She then ran from the house.

It was now left to Priscilla Fallas to get hold of Hammond's hand and say: 'Don't Billy'.

As she was pushed away she saw her uncle bring the blade down on the old man's head – her grandfather was still sitting in a rocking chair. Mrs Fallas then ran from the house shouting: 'Thou will know about this Billy – thal get hung for it.'

Immediately outside was an 18-year-old colliery jenny boy, by the name of Herbert Harry Baxter. At Mrs Fallas's request, he ran into the house to see the old man, still seated and bleeding from his throat. He was saying: 'Don't Billy – look what tha's done,' but his silent son brought the knife down once again and blood, 'about an inch thick', gushed from the wound. The old man dropped his hand to his knees and bent forward.

Apparently noticing Baxter for the first time, Hammond kept the knife raised and drove him from the house into the yard. The youth subsequently described Hammond as looking 'like a madman', and added, 'I think he would have struck me if I had stood still'.

Seconds later Mrs Fallas returned to the house with neighbour Mrs Frances Gawthorpe to find the old man stooping over the sink and bleeding heavily.

As Mrs Fallas ran for a bed sheet, he turned to Mrs Gawthorpe and said:

'See, Fanny, what our Billy's done to me.'

A crowd of people had gained entrance to the house by the time Billy Hammond returned. Still armed with the knife, he announced:

'You must all go out or I shall make you.'

He had, however, not reckoned on neighbours Thomas Brannan and Tom Glover. Brannan's reply was: 'I won't'. As Hammond squared up for a fight, Brannan struck him and knocked him against the sink.

Both men then disarmed him and sat him on a chair near the door. Rising to his feet as if to leave, Hammond then said, 'Let me be I'll put an end to it, I'll drown myself'. Asked why had had done it, he then rubbed his head saying it was 'bad' and adding, 'This is what done it, I cut my head at Barrow pit twelve months ago and have never been right since.'

He repeated those words several times.

William Hammond senior was in a state of collapse by the time the police and medical help arrived. He was taken by motor car to Barnsley Beckett Hospital but died without recovering consciousness two hours later. The cause of death was shock and haemorrhage following four knife wounds, a long one to the scalp and neck, another long one to the neck and cheek and smaller ones to his nose and hand.

Billy Hammond was charged with attempted murder the same evening and with wilful murder the following day. Monday morning saw him appear at the West Riding Magistrates' Court at Barnsley on the latter charge at which time he sported a black eye. Apart from that he was described as 'respectable looking' and 'maintaining a quiet demeanor'.

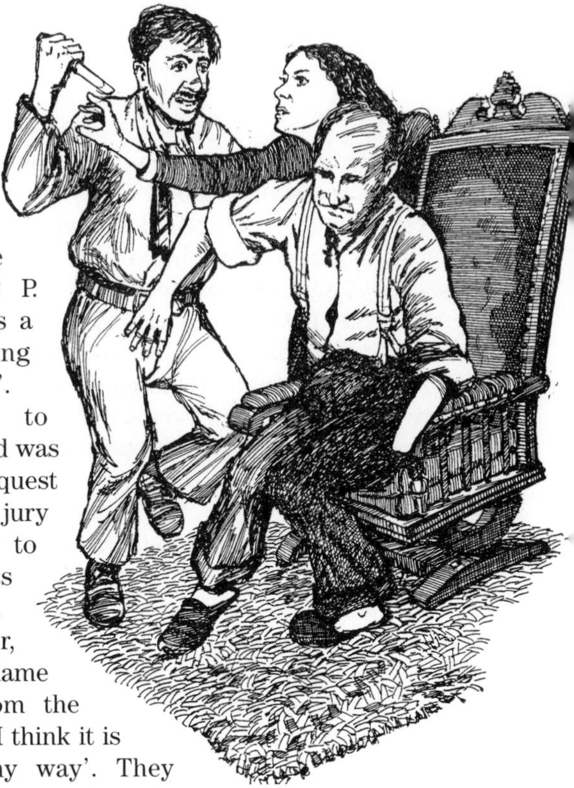

The inquest was opened the same day, but adjourned until the Thursday after the district coroner, Mr P. P. Maitland, described it as a 'shocking case requiring very careful examination'.

No evidence as to Hammond's state of mind was heard at the resumed inquest and the Coroner told the jury they were there simply to establish the facts surrounding the death. The jury did, however, hear Mrs Hammond blame herself for running from the house, saying tearfully: 'I think it is I who have missed my way'. They subsequently returned from a five-minute retirement, with a verdict of wilful murder against Hammond.

The prisoner was described as 'haggard and pale, but outwardly calm', at his next appearance before the magistrates, when Mrs Hammond told the court that they lived 'comfortably', despite the fact that her husband had not worked for the past 25 years. The family had been maintained during those years by Billy, a bachelor, and his two brothers. Despite his son being a major breadwinner, William Hammond had often been abusive towards him.

Asked if her husband was quarrelsome, Mrs Hammond said:

'He was indeed, he could not agree with himself, he couldn't really.'

Mrs Hammond added that her son could do nothing right for his father, even when he had had nothing to drink. She then told the court about her son being involved in the rock fall at Barrow Colliery in November, 1910. Following that, she said, he rarely slept for more than an hour, often complained of 'bumping in his head' and had complained that he could no longer read a newspaper.

Mrs Hammond added that her son had also stated that drink no longer agreed with him and he was thinking of 'signing teetotal'. She also told the court that he was not as pleasant as he used to be.

It was at this hearing that the family doctor, a Dr Beverley, said the colliery accident had resulted in a depression of Hammond's skull large enough to admit the tip of a first finger. He said it was possible that the skull was pressing on the brain and this could account for slight brain trouble.

But when Dr Beverley gave evidence at the Leeds Assize Court hearing, before Mr Justice Horridge, on January 31, he said there was no pressure on the brain from the bone. He also said that, while he had treated Hammond since the accident, he had never discovered any symptoms of his being even minutely affected it.

That evidence was damning to the case of defence counsel Mr Charles Mellor, who was acting under instructions from Barnsley solicitor Mr Raley. He had not disputed the facts of the case, but sought to stress witness accounts that Hammond had acted like a 'madman'. The 'not guilty' plea failed. The jury returned a verdict of 'guilty', but sought permission to add a recommendation to mercy.

The judge welcomed that recommendation and added that he would see it was forwarded to the proper quarter, then sentenced Hammond to death.

The resultant petition for clemency was organised by Hammond's solicitors and signed by Barnsley's Mayor, Coun. J. H. Cotterill and other civic leaders. Signatures were also collected in Worsbrough and Stairfoot as well as the Chronicle offices. It was a lengthy document, chronicling the mitigating features of the case and a striking contrast to the touching letter written to the Home Secretary by Mrs Hammond. Part of which read:

'I am a heartbroken woman. My husband has gone and my son is in a condemned cell. I am old, Sir, and ill but if I could only take his place and sacrifice my life for his, I would gladly do it.'

Thankfully such a sacrifice was not required.

William Hammond was buried in St Thomas's churchyard, Worsbrough – just yards away from the monument in memory of the 143 men and boys, killed in an explosion at Swaithe Main Colliery on December 6th, 1875, at which time, Hammond was employed there.

His gravestone, if he had ever had one, is one of those which does not appear to have survived the passing of time.

Victim: ***John Brook, fatal punch,* April 1913**

John Brook was no stranger to fights, his 65 years of life being spent in a mining area during the Victorian and Edwardian eras. In those days life was hard and fights were frequent. By April, 1913, John Brook (sometimes spelt with a final 'e'), was not only elderly, but had been partially crippled in a mining accident. He depended on a stick to get about and hardly seems likely to have offered to fight a man 42 years his junior.

That, however, is exactly what a Leeds Assize Court jury were asked to believe.

Fred Bevan, a 23-year-old miner was appearing before them, indicted with the manslaughter of Mr Brook. He took his place in the witness box and informed the court that the aged Mr Brook had not only started an argument between them but, in addition, offered to fight him for five shillings.

His claim was such that Mr Justice Darling felt it necessary to interpose. Addressing Bevan's counsel, Mr S. Fleming, the learned judge said:

'I should like to know what defence there is in this case.'

Mr Fleming replied that their case centred on provocation. He said Bevan formed the view that Brook was going to strike him and so got his blow in first, the blow which caused Brook's death. In his view he proclaimed, it was not manslaughter.

The judge does not appear to have been too impressed by this line of reasoning. In his summing up to the jury, he said that there was nothing to have prevented Bevan from walking away, if he didn't want to fight. With that in mind, the jury returned from their retirement with a verdict that Bevan was guilty of manslaughter but recommended mercy on account of his youth.

Asked if he had anything to add, Bevan told the court he was very sorry for what he had done and further added that he had a father, a wife and two children to support.

The judge then sentenced him to three months' imprisonment saying he had struck the old man a blow and then 'callously' turned round and left him to die. Those court proceedings were the sequel to an incident which took place at the Hammer and Anvil public house, Station Road, Ryhill, on April 8th, 1913. It was around 5.30 p.m. when John Brook walked into the hostelry. Already in the tap room were a small number of men, including Fred Bevan.

Mr Brook was sober having spent all day in Barnsley in an attempt to secure some compensation pay, which was due because of an injury he had received at Hodroyd Colliery in January, 1912. The accident had resulted in Brook being restricted to light work only and he had felt unable to continue doing even that just nine weeks previously.

Brook, now relying on a stick, told those assembled that his compensation quest had been in vain and he intended repeating the mission the following day.

Who suggested the game of dominoes is not exactly clear, but shortly after his arrival Mr Brook and Bevan were playing a game.

The next those present heard was an argument between the two men. Both rose to their feet and then Bevan punched Brook violently in the face with his fist. The old man fell to the stone floor. His head struck it with a jarring thud. Brook was bleeding from the nose and mouth and appeared to be unconscious, but rallied after treatment in the pub's kitchen. Eventually he told his helpers that he wanted to go home. Bevan, by this time, was preparing to leave the pub. John Taylor, a miner, of Brick Row, Ryhill, immediately approached him and told him he had done wrong. Bevan walked outside without replying and then ran off quickly in the direction of his home.

Arthur Holt, a miner who lived near the Hammer and Anvil and sometimes waited-on there, volunteered to walk Mr Brook to his house in Reginald Terrace. Brook wasn't speaking clearly en route, but was independent enough to ask Holt not to hold his arm.

Mr Brook arrived home at around 6 p.m. He looked as though he had lost a lot of blood and told his wife he didn't know how his injuries had occurred, because he was 'knocked' until he didn't know. He asked his wife to help him undress him and get him to bed. While doing so she noticed a large swelling and cut to the back of his head but she still didn't think it necessary to summon a doctor.

Mr Brook died at 7 a.m. the following morning having spent a lot of the night moaning and asking his wife to rub his head.

Fred Bevan was arrested later the same day and charged with

manslaughter. He made no reply. On the Friday, he appeared before the inquest held at Ryhill's Wesleyan School. He heard Dr Lister, of Sandal, say that death was due to an effusion of blood in the brain following a fracture to the skull.

The district coroner, Mr P. P. Maitland, told the jury they had no alternative but to return a verdict of manslaughter against Bevan, if they were satisfied that Brook's death was the result of falling from a blow struck by him. The revelation that Brook had been involved in a number of fights throughout his life, came to light at a commital hearing before the West Riding Magistrates Court at Barnsley.

Mr Brook's widow was asked if her husband was quarrelsome by nature. Her answer was, 'He was quiet if they would let him be quiet'. Asked if he had been involved in fights, she said, 'Yes, he has had fights many a time', and continued, 'if crossed when in drink, he would be in a bad temper'. She added, however, that her husband didn't get drunk regularly, although he did like a glass of beer.

A procession of witnesses was called to give evidence about the game of dominoes, all said they believed it was a friendly game with

no financial stakes and neither man was drunk. Each witnessin turn was cross-examined by Bevan's solicitor, Mr C. A. White, as to whether he had seen five shillings on the table and Holt was asked whether it was a custom of the house to play dominoes to determine who bought the drinks. A question which the clerk of the court instructed Holt not to answer, for obvious reasons.

Apparently tired with that line of cross-examination, Superindent McDonald then told the court that none of the prosecution witnesses could remember five shillings being placed on the table. 'As a matter of fact,' he added, 'the deceased had to pawn his watch to raise the rail fare to get to Barnsley.'

The reason for that line of cross-examination became obvious when the defence called Mr William Williamson, a miner of Monckton Row, Royston. Williamson told the court he had seen Bevan playing dominoes with an unknown man, Bevan won the game but the man wouldn't pay for the drinks. Then, he said, an older man offered to play Bevan. Bevan won that game as well, but the old man wouldn't pay. The old man then said he would fight Bevan for 5s.

When warned by the clerk about the importance of his evidence, Williamson then seemed to backtrack. He agreed that the older man was aged about 65, but then added that he was bearded, John Brook was clean-shaven. And when asked if the older man was the man who was killed, he replied: 'I am sure I cannot say, I wasn't in the room when the blow was struck.'

Bevan was committed to stand trial for manslaughter at Leeds Assize Court. An application for bail was refused despite his father and other relatives offering to 'stand' for him, the rest you already know.

John Brook died for a trivial reason, an argument about a game of dominoes. Sixteen months later a war of global proportions was to break out and millions of men were to lay down their lives in what they believed was a struggle for freedom.

Whether Fred Bevan played his part in that epic confrontation is not known, it is known that his name is not among the 39 men from Ryhill and Havercroft whose memory is honoured at the war memorial in Ryhill Cemetery.

Acknowledgements

Barnsley Library Local Studies
York City Library
The Barnsley Chronicle
The South Yorkshire Times
Alfred O Elmhirst
Willie Frith
Denys Corrigan
Donald Harrison
Leonard Burland

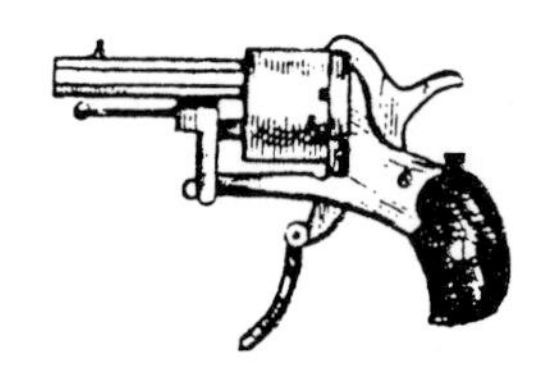